Behind My American Dream
A Story of Opportunities and Disappointments

by

Maggie Zurowska

Edited by Catherine Gigante-Brown
Cover and interior design by Vinnie Corbo

Published by Volossal Publishing
www.volossal.com

Copyright © 2024
ISBN 978-1-963359-15-2

This book may not be reproduced or resold in whole or in part through print, electronic or any other medium. All rights reserved.

Table of Contents

Introduction	5
Chapter One - UC Davis 2022	7
Chapter Two - Au Pair	9
Chapter Three - The First of Everything	17
Chapter Four - Family Values	27
Chapter Five - Professional Sitter	43
Chapter Six - Serving is Fun!	55
Chapter Seven - Office Failure	69
Chapter Eight - A Tour Guide Career	79
Chapter Nine - More Opportunities—and Failures	95
Chapter Ten - A College Career	101
Chapter Eleven - Behind My American Dream	113
Chapter Twelve - What's Cooking?	119
Chapter Thirteen - New Dream, New Destination	127
Epilogue	141
Acknowledgements	143
About the Author	145

Introduction

Many people travel to the United States to escape from a difficult life in their home countries. They live every day in fear of being killed, raped or threatened by gangs. The lucky ones manage to cross the border to the promised land, the United States of America. Others come to the US chasing their big "American Dream." Those dreams are driven by promises of freedom and opportunities in a country where everyone can make it if they just try. I imagine that, just like me, Frank Sinatra's song pops up in their heads as they arrive in New York: "If I can make it there, I'll make it anywhere!" But little do they know that their big American dream could easily turn into an American Nightmare.

This story is mine and mine alone. The tale of an Eastern European immigrant, who, through different jobs, experienced a journey of success and failures in the USA. It's about learning and growing while seeking opportunities. But whether my path is bumpy or filled with flowers, I've found the road a way of discovering what is most important in life.

This is my American Dream story. Have fun! I'm glad you're along for the ride!

Chapter One
UC Davis 2022

It's 2022 at the University of California, Davis (UC Davis), exactly 20 years since I arrived at the United States. I'm at UC Davis, near Sacramento, but not as a student. I work here. Within these two decades, I have traveled a long way to get where I am now. And not just geographically. This place has totally changed my life and my understanding of what success is. I have worked many jobs, struggling to climb the Ladder of Success, and it has brought me to this point. Basically, I watch coffee.

Although I work at UC Davis, I'm not sure why I do what I do. I'm not a professor, not even an administrative worker. My job: to watch a coffee station in one of the student dining rooms. Yes, my position is "front of the house" service and my responsibility specifically focuses on maintaining the beverage stations, refilling coffee, water and other drinks.

When you see me circling the dining room replenishing coffee, it might look like I'm doing practically nothing, but the truth is I'm extremely busy. My mind is overloaded with thoughts. For one, I'm planning—planning a protest in my head. In between coffee refills, I'm also writing texts to people who can help the cause. The protest is against UC Davis, the place where I am currently employed.

You see, besides us workers and students, there are other warm-blooded beings at the university. The difference is that it's not their choice to be here; they are prisoners. Their reality is dark, painful and full of fear, with no future for them at all. "Them" being the thousands of animals at one of the country's largest primate research centers. Which happens to be at UC Davis.

Every day countless weak and powerless animals are tortured here. It's difficult to believe that in 2022, we still conduct these tests on vulnerable, warm-blooded creatures when there are other alternatives.

Do I like my job? Of course not. But I do learn a lot. Just by being here and listening to these terrible animal cruelty stories, my vision of the American Dream has changed. I have a new purpose in life, a new focus.

But first, let me backtrack.

Chapter Two
Au Pair

My story begins in 2002 Poland. While researching a way to spend my gap year before grad school, my best friend, Justina, introduces me to an international program called Au Pair. Magnetized by the alluring name, I decide to investigate more about what exactly an Au Pair is. Sifting through Google pages, I quickly learn that the fancy French term is simply a babysitting exchange program. *Voilla!*

Perfect! I think. This can easily be me! Traveling to somewhere, anywhere, to an exciting, unknown place is amazing. Since I already speak English (but not well!), I pick the United States where the program is very popular. Originally, I was looking for an exchange student program with the possibility of making money and learning about a different culture. But the Au Pair position is even more than I'd hoped for. The chance to practice my English and visit new places sweetens the pot. Plus, I would get to escape my reality. I need a break from my busy university life. I want to explore the world—and on someone else's dime. It looks like this Au Pair program has it all.

I figure that I can easily become a babysitter since I already have some experience with elementary school kids. During middle school, I was a scout leader and looked after my friends who were not much younger than myself. However, I don't have much experience with babies, a skill the Au Pair program specifies. What's more, I am afraid of being saddled with nightmarish, non-stop crying creatures. I wouldn't know what to do with them!

The image of holding a screaming "it" in my arms is way beyond my comfort zone. It scares me to death. Growing up, as the younger sister, I was always the baby, the one being taken care of. I always got what I wanted, even though my expectations were put in check many times. But I always found a way to get my heart's desire. I never had to worry about someone else. As the youngest one, I only learned how to misbehave. Maybe I'm afraid I'd have a cunning little brat like me to look after!

But I don't let my Au Pair fears stop me. I never let fear stop me! Besides, the Au Pair phenomenon is having a heyday in 2002 America. And I am determined to ride that wave. Where the riches are, there's also a need for service, and people are willing to pay for that service. I am about to learn this firsthand.

I'm surprised to discover that the fancy French term, Au Pair, has little to do with what it is. I soon learn that people in the US actually want us to sound British. Maybe this is a "Mary Poppins" fantasy—because she was perhaps the most famous, magical Au Pair of them all.

The job already sounds intriguing—and complicated. Will I be able to adapt to life in the US? Will I be good at looking after children? Despite my doubts, I am excited about the whole notion of being paid for travel, English-language courses and housing on top of earning a bit of pocket money. But spending a whole year in a foreign country babysitting strangers' kids in a cultural environment unlike my own…hey, that's a long time.

Chapter Two - Au Pair

It's not as though I haven't done my share of traveling before. Living in a post-communist country like Poland, the borders had been closed during much of my childhood. The oppressive communist system didn't allow us to see the beautiful reality on the other side of the Iron Curtain. (I.e. freedom, democracy.) When communism finally collapsed in 1989 and the borders opened, I made my first international trip at ten years old. It was so exciting to travel, and not just around Poland anymore. But abroad!

That trip, we went as far as Slovakia, a neighboring country 30 miles away. Slovakia didn't feel exotic since they spoke a similar language and shared a similar culture. We pretended not to understand the Slovaks to make it seem like we were sophisticated, international travelers from a faraway land. But in reality, we were very alike.

Everything looked the same in Slovakia. Crude and gray. I imagined that further to the west, the surroundings were fancier, brighter. On our first trip out of Poland, we only toured the Slovakian mountains, visiting old cathedrals and castles. But still, it opened a gate to the Western World, which I had the opportunity to explore later. I made several other trips, venturing further each time. All the way to Egypt, Israel and even to the United States.

Whenever I had the chance to escape and explore, I took it. I longed to go somewhere, anywhere, as long as it was far away. But the trips were always short. Nowhere near a year's commitment. I always came back home after a few weeks.

But I know being an Au Pair will be different. I can feel it in my bones. Somehow, I know my time as an Au Pair in the US would be a life changer. And it is.

•

Back in the eighties, when Poland was still under the communist regime, my father had the opportunity to travel to the United States. He brought back home with him the wave of Western capitalism and prosperity in the form of a banana and chewing gum. Bananas were a symbol of freedom to most of us in Eastern Europe. So tropical, so exotic. I remember that this single banana my dad brought us was still green. We had to wait for it to ripen before before we could taste it...like the freedom we had to wait a little longer to achieve.

But at the time, the banana—and chocolate drinks, packets of colorful chewing gum, stickers and brightly-colored pencils—was a breath of fresh air. A taste of the forbidden fruit, literally. This banana is one of my most profound childhood memories. Never before had I been given so many bright, pretty things at once.

For instance, I had to wait ages to get my bicycle. Most of my clothes were hand-me-downs that were worn out by the time I got them. Not only did my sister wear them before me, practically the whole town did too! Only, these treasures from America...they were shiny and new and all mine.

Under communism, it was hard, if not impossible, to buy most things. And it was almost unimaginable to get luxury items without connections. Having friends who could procure things on the Black Market was like having a golden ticket in *Charlie and the Chocolate Factory*.

Instead of money, Poles had "portion cards," which were slips of paper used to procure our monthly limited ration of an item. For example, you could get sugar, candy or other "goodies," but only if they were available in the store. Most of the time, they weren't offered or else they were reserved for someone else, commonly a communist party representative.

My family was lucky. We received clothing and other items from the underground group that supported solidarity movement members like my parents. We passed around the same toys, clothes and other necessary goods between us. So, we wore used clothes and played with used toys. They were often broken or mended over and over again. It was a rare luxury to have a brand-new item.

New things were only available in a store called "Pewex." It offered commodities not normally available for purchase in other stores. This included technological items like computers as well as furniture and luxury items like alcohol, quality cigarettes and candy. Because these things came from the West, anything for sale in the Pewex store was expensive. Plus, they only dealt in dollars. (In Cuba, I believe they called them "dollar stores.") Pewex was an exclusive place. Just a select few people had access to it. Again, mostly communist party collaborators. The store became a symbol of privilege. But that was the reality back then in pre-1989 Poland. Everyone tried to find a way to survive.

But back to the banana! Having it was a luxury. It lifted my status among my friends. Having a banana (and all the treasures my dad brought back from the West) was also like being a magnet. All my neighbors and school friends were drawn to me and wanted to be my best buddy. My disappointment came later when I ran out of shiny things and discovered that it was not about me and friendship but about the banana. It mattered more to them, not me. Looking back, I can't blame people for wanting something they couldn't have. Instead, I blame the system for keeping those things away from us.

You might be wondering why (and how!) my dad was able to travel to the United States in the 1980s when Polish borders were closed. Many Poles emigrated to the US through the United Kingdom and brought their families, who could then apply for visas. My cousin was one of those people. He was in the US and invited my father to visit. Since my dad was an active solidarity movement member, the Polish communist government was more than happy to send Dad abroad. Probably hoping he wouldn't come back! But he did—bearing gifts.

•

Decades later, when presented with the opportunity to be an Au Pair in America, I wonder, *Is this how it will be in the States? Will the disappointment of owning something but not having a real friend come back to haunt me when I'm there?* I will soon see.

This is how my early childhood memories of the West stain my mind. Material wealth equals having friends. I'm afraid of getting disappointed again by shiny, meaningless things that determine one's position in society but provide no warmth or nourishment. I am aware that US society is hyper focused on commercialism and material wealth. The almighty dollar determines social status in the US, when in Poland, it's your family heritage, history and origin that dictates who you are. This would gradually change with the influence from the West, however. But in 2002, it was still important.

I am more than ready to explore a different culture. I'm excited—and honestly, scared—about my upcoming year in the States.

•

"When asked, 'How are you?,' always say, 'I'm okay!' and smile. They like that over there," my Auntie Basia, a world traveler, advises. She is giving me pointers on how to survive in America. Being the wife of a journalist and a diplomat, Auntie Basia not only has traveled the world but knows all the successful techniques and necessary performance requirements diplomacy requires. These things not only make a positive impression on people but gives them what they want, Aunt Basia schools. At least pretend if you lack confidence because "If you fake it, you will make it!" This is what Auntie Basia adds at the end of our pep talk before my imminent departure.

And fake it, I do!

My bags are already packed, waiting for me in a corner of my room. I just need one more important thing to add to my work profile: photographs of me with babies, not only with elementary school kids. The pictures will provide physical evidence that I'm qualified for the Au Pair position and increase my chances of getting a better babysitting offer.

I have photos taken with an adorable one-year-old boy I am temporarily looking after. This temp job is thanks to my resourceful friend Justina. She's helping her friend, a young mother, take care of her little one. Justina comes up with the brilliant idea for me to babysit the child for a couple of days. To break me in, so to speak. This way, I'll get experience with young kids and Justina will take pics to prove my babysitting skills. Not thinking twice, I'm in!

I thoroughly enjoy my two days babysitting Mark, a sweet blonde-haired, blue-eyed boy. In that short time, I learn a lot and now have a folder full of photo ops that scream of my experience. The final step in the Au Pair process is actually applying for the job.

•

Lidia, who runs the Warsaw branch of the international Au Pair program, is impressed by my experience, especially with elementary and middle school kids. She comments, "You have potential. I love your profile." What Lidia loves most about me is that I'm extremely active—I do all sorts of sports—and that I've traveled a lot. With my experience skiing, scuba diving, hiking and such, she says I'm the perfect Au Pair candidate. On top of that, I'm adventurous and liberal-minded.

"There's only one problem," Lidia admits. "We can't include these pictures in your folder." She points out two with Mark. "Nobody in the States wants to see a half-naked child taking a bath. It's considered a crime there." Little did I know that my "brilliant" idea of taking pics with a kid in the bathtub was illegal in the US. That's my first cultural surprise and I haven't even traveled to America yet!

After my meeting with Lidia, I go home and study more about child safety and the dangers (real or imagined) lurking in every corner. I decide to become the best babysitter ever. A friend, a protector and guard dog, if necessary.

Chapter Three
The First of Everything

I made it! I'm here and living my dream!
That's my first thought when I arrive at my destination. But not two minutes earlier, I was still up in the night sky, thinking I was going to die. And not because I have a fear of flying. Blame it on jet lag but looking down on the incredibly bright illuminations below filled me with a strange feeling. I studied what appeared to be millions of colorful lights spreading out in an endless spider web. To me, it looked as though all the lights existed in an alien dimension, stretching for the sky. Like the Tower of Babel from the Bible. Does this tower of light hide sinners speaking many languages? Do these sinners run in different directions, not knowing how to communicate with each other? Will I become one of them too?

Scary thoughts, for sure, but I still can't resist the beauty of the lights. I'm a moth drawn into the splendor of brightness. I fear that these alluring lights might become my own worst enemy, and in the end, pull me inside and destroy me. I'm afraid to fall into the abyss. To calm down, I convince myself that these lights resemble Christmas tree decorations back home. I tell myself they're the kind of tiny, colorful holiday lights that give you a cozy, warm feeling inside. As I fly closer to the spray of lights, I know it isn't a Christmas tree or the Tower of Babel. It's a breathtaking nighttime view of New York City in all its glory.

As I land at John F. Kennedy International Airport, my phone doesn't stop ringing. Weirdly enough, the last few days in Poland, I receive numerous calls from prospective families from all over the US. The agency informs me that this is not the usual vetting process. The typical selection method is for one family to call at a time. Then both the family and the Au Pair candidate decide whether they're a match. If there's no connection, then another family will contact you for an interview. Those are the rules but that's not what happens with me!

I think my well-padded profile causes a wave of simultaneous phone calls from desperate potential families at the last minute. After the initial interviews, I decide to go with a New York-based, Korean-Jewish family. They have two elementary school-aged kids, a boy and a girl. But to me, it doesn't really matter how old they are or who they are. The important thing is the location: New York City.

I can't believe that I'm landing in the infamous metropolis I've seen in movies, heard about in songs and read about in books. I touch down in "the city that never sleeps" in the middle of the night at one of the busiest airports in the world, JFK.

I'm probably in shock because it takes me a while to leave the plane. The excitement overwhelms me and I keep forgetting my stuff. On top of that, people are moving slowly, sleepwalking. Part of me wants to prod them to move faster and the other part wants to politely excuse myself and cut ahead. But I find myself paralyzed. I can't say a word. I'm afraid to open my mouth and speak English. For some reason, I feel ashamed and just can't.

Chapter Three - The First of Everything

Help comes in the form of a flight attendant who, sensing the situation, appears with a comforting smile, and asks, "Are you okay?"

My Aunt Basia's words ring in my head. Like a Kalashnikov rifle, I shoot out the answer, "Yes, ma'am, I'm okay."

The flight attendant responds with an even bigger grin. "You can go now. The doors are open." Her words—and her dazzling smile—comfort me. I am ready. I excuse myself, pass the slow pokes crowding the aisle, and finally leave the plane to meet my destiny.

At Passport Control, I encounter a small roadblock. The immigration officer who interviews me acts as if I've committed a crime—or am about to. In a threatening voice, he asks if I'm carrying any food—like kielbasa. I step back, shocked. My mouth hangs open. *Racist much?* I think. Even though I'm worried he won't let me into the country, I stand tall, look him in the eye and in a strong voice, tell him, "No."

•

My host is waiting on the other side of Passport Control. He welcomes me with a large sign that has my name written on it—Maggie Zurowska—and a warm smile. "Hi, I'm John. Welcome to New York!" he says.

You certainly don't get a welcoming feeling while passing through Customs, I think. "Hi," I respond. "It was a long flight but there was an amazing view at the end. It was worth it."

"You're lucky to land at night," he says. "How was Passport Control? No issues?"

I decide not to tell him about the prejudiced immigration agent. "Lovely!" I answer sarcastically.

"You got through Customs fast," John tells me. "There are five more of your friends joining us who were on the same flight. We need to wait for them. Why don't you take a seat and relax." Sitting down is the last thing I want to do after my 10-hour flight! I decide to stretch and walk around. Fascinated by the assortment of people surrounding me, I get lost in time.

Maybe 30 minutes pass. John waves from across the airport. When I get closer, he tells me that we're ready to board the bus. *What does he mean?* I wonder. *Where is he taking me? Is he going to kidnap me and sell me into white slavery? Is there something I missed about the program? Maybe I didn't get it right because of my poor English. Or maybe the Au Pair program is a coverup for something else!*

Overall, my English is not so great. I know phrases like "Thank you "and "Okay," maybe a couple more. I can communicate, not easily, but I can still communicate. "It's Orientation Week" John informs me. "First, you get accustomed to the program, then we place you with your host family. Remember?"

"Oh right!" I tell him, relieved I'm not being groomed for a life of prostitution. Phew, I'm safe! "Thanks, John. I forgot. It's just the long flight. I'm tired and a little overwhelmed."

"No problem! Just jump on the bus. We're ready to go. And please, don't worry about anything," he assures me.

We're on the highway an hour already and haven't seen much of New York City. Just peeks of faraway buildings and the many bridges we cross. The bus is full of girls and only two guys. Maybe they're babysitters too? For some reason, the thought of males babysitting makes me laugh. Sexist, I know. I'm so beat that my brain is playing tricks on me. I'm exhausted beyond being able to sleep but exhaustion still doesn't stop my silly thoughts. Or maybe it's the sheer happiness of being in the United States that's making me giddy. But something in the air causes me to smile. A lot.

I check around to see if it's just me. It isn't. Everyone else looks exhausted but excited about the whole experience. Nobody talks. Our eyes are glued to the

Chapter Three - The First of Everything

windows, trying to catch a glimpse of New York. We all know that these earliest impressions of the Big Apple will stay with us forever, so we savor them.

The glare of the city lights in the dark and the motion of the bus ride finally puts me to sleep. I wake up, just as the bus arrives at a hotel. But we're not in New York anymore, I notice. We're in a neighboring state called Connecticut. It looks nice, at least from the bus. Fancy for my Eastern European taste, but still nice. At this point, I don't really care, though. I'm happy to go straight to my room where I can finally relax after this long, draining day.

There are hundreds of us Au Pairs at the modern-looking Connecticut hotel. Babysitters from all over the world. It reminds me of a page from *The Handmaid's Tale*. We're all gathered in the same place for the same purpose. Truthfully, it's a bit awkward, but it still feels terrific to be surrounded by this League of Nations speaking several tongues. We are diverse in nationality but united in the notion of being away from home for the entire year. You can feel the exhilaration sizzling in the air.

All of us are in our early 20s, ready to explore the alternate reality we've invented for ourselves. We share the same goal—improving our English, becoming independent and free, away from home. Wherever "home" happens to be. New York City…a brave, new world. It's waiting for us! We want to conquer it!

The place we all know from the movies was always like a dream to us. It appears so vivid and magical on film, yet here we all are, finally in the Promised Land! In New York, anyone can become anything they want. You can become invisible in the crowds or you can be "seen." With so many opportunities, you can even become someone else. To me, New York City is a symbol of freedom and self-indulgence. I so want to become part of it but for now, I'm stuck in an anonymous hotel in the wilds of Connecticut. For the time being, this will have to do.

When I open the door to my room, I see a huge mess. Suitcases and clothes litter almost every surface. The medium-sized room is equipped with two big beds and still manages to look comfy in spite of the chaos. Someone sleeps soundly in one bed. A blanket is pulled all the way up to their ears. Only part of their head peeking out. Long, dark hair sprawls on the fluffy pillow.

When I close the door behind me, the head on the pillow moves. Large, dark, tired eyes stare back at me. Soon after the eyes, a mouth becomes visible. It's a human being! A sleepy but friendly voice says, "Hey! My name is Joys. We're roommates. I'm Brazilian and you?" I soon learn that Joys is very proud of her nationality. But she's also curious about mine. Joys slowly rises and stretches her shapely legs and slender arms. Even messy, Joys looks cool and super attractive. She's exactly the way us Eastern Europeans, imagine exotic, young Brazilian girls to be. Joys resembles a slinky, sexy Rio carnival dancer with her flowing black hair, bronze skin, big, brown eyes and an even bigger smile. Joys looks flawless, like a Barbie doll. But the South American version, hot-blooded, with more character.

After sizing up Joys, I tell her, "I'm Polish. My name is Maggie and I just arrived." There's an awkward silence so I continue yapping, nervous and excited. "It looks like you had a good sleep. I'm sorry to wake you. I need to sleep too but I'm so excited I can't settle down yet."

"Yeah, it's exciting but I'm exhausted too," Joys admits. "Traveling from Brazil takes a long time. I'm trying to get in a short nap before orientation starts. This bed is sooo soft. You should give it a try and get some rest."

My bed is closer to the bathroom than Joys's bed is. The gigantic mattress is much larger than what we have in Poland. I remember hearing that everything in the US is double the size of everything in Europe. Americans supposedly like enormous things!

Again, I'm reminded of what I noticed before: owning oversized things makes people feel important and determines their status. Honestly, I'm so tired that I can't give it much thought. All I want to do is dive into that big, fat American bed. I learn that the biggest bed here is called a "king size." It's so humongous that it *does* make you feel like royalty. As if you're a monarch in a castle surrounded by an army of pillows. And peons.

Without changing into my pajamas, I jump into the bed. I slowly drift off to sleep, thinking about how I'm already loving it here in the US as I disappear into a cloud of softness.

•

"Never, never shake a baby!"
"Call 911 when something is wrong with a child!"
"Learn the house rules!"

I'm jolted awake by a loud set of instructions being yelled at me. Or am I still dreaming? Since my arrival, everything seems surreal. I pinch myself. It hurts, which means it's real and I'm still awake. Welcome to my first day of orientation. I must have drifted off.

The six-hour time difference between Poland and Connecticut is killing me. I'm afraid I'll forget what I learned in orientation. I'm a zombie with jetlag, barely acknowledging the voices blaring around me.

"Always be careful when driving with kids and never forget to stop at a stop sign!"

Karen, the supervisor who welcomed us to the hotel upon arrival, is now navigating us through the Au Pair program guidelines. She's tall with short blonde hair and a nice smile. Karen looks trustworthy, someone you'd go to with your problems. She speaks slowly, loudly and firmly, which makes me feel that my English is perfect.

(PS, it isn't!) I understand almost 100% of what Karen says. This feeds my ego and my self-esteem rises like a hot air balloon.

The warnings during our Au Pair training come fast and furious:

"Remember, never overstay your valid one-year work visa."

"Don't forget, after September 11, immigration laws are much more strict."

That's right, it's August 2002, almost a year after the September 11th attacks and the US is still on high alert. I feel so sad about what happened in New York City, Pennsylvania and Washington, DC. As a European with a history rich in wars, I can empathize and feel people's pain. The ache of 9/11 is still very much alive in America. I feel sad that I never had a chance to see the iconic Twin Towers, which were destroyed by terrorists less than a year before my visit. I wander off into gloomy thoughts, but just for a moment. I force myself to focus on the future instead of the past and try to find the positive in even in an incredibly horrific situation. I've been told this is the Americans way—they don't forget what happened (because remembrance is important) but at the same time, they try to move forward.

Us Europeans carry all the drama of the past with us; we don't know how to look into the future with optimism. Instead, we constantly cry over the past, at least in Poland. I feel that Poles fixate on the past too much, celebrate it, even. Frankly, I'm tired of it.

As a symbol of moving forward, my credo will now be: "I'm leaving my European sadness behind and stepping into American happiness." That will be my mantra on this trip, I decide. Well, in addition to all the other babysitting chants they keep throwing at us.

Like this latest one: "Always stay positive, everything can be fixed."

This is the closing thought Karen, our supervisor, offers us. I don't know about my comrades, but my head is swimming with supposedly helpful but mostly terrifying philosophies.

Chapter Four
Family Values

Finally, the day to meet my host family arrives. By now, us Au Pairs are well trained and are looking forward to seeing our hosts in the flesh for the first time. Before this, we only spoke to them on the telephone once or twice. We never actually "saw" each other. (Remember, Zoom wasn't a thing back in 2002.) Oh, they sent us photos, but ultimately, I think people look different in person than they do in pictures. Flatter. Less real.

I still have a few more hours before the Hams pick me up, so I try to make the most of my last moments of freedom. I savor my last breakfast with my newfound friends, my last hugs. We snap group pics and before you know it, it's time to pack. It's tough gathering my stuff. I'm full of tears for my new buddies—I miss them already. I've always found goodbyes hard and this is no exception. We promise to get together as much as possible, but will we?

All of us have grown close these past few days together. As soon as we leave the hotel, we'll be relocated to various parts of the US, New York and beyond.

During our training, we share rooms, stories lavish hotel dinners, and talk long into the night. We bond. It's tough to believe it's already time to say goodbye. The days passed so quickly.

I have mixed feelings about moving on. I'm excited about my upcoming adventures but sad about leaving my new friends behind.

Suddenly, I hear someone calling my name. Maggie, my new American name, not my Polish name, which is too long and convoluted for American tongues. My birth name, "Malgorzata," can be translated as "Margaret." But I think "Margaret" sounds too serious, too formal. "Margarita," like the drink, sounds too trivial for the professional babysitting role I'm about to play. So, Maggie I become.

"Maggie!" Here it is again. I look toward the sound of my new name, my new life, and prepare to meet my new American host family.

Hmmm, they don't really resemble the picture they sent me. In it, they are all wearing the same Santa sweaters. (I thought this odd, since they're a Korean-Jewish family and supposedly don't celebrate Christmas.) Thankfully, the pasted-on smiles and funny-looking clothing don't determine my Au Pair choice. No, the idea of being part of a mixed, multicultural family attracted me to the Hams. I thought they were characteristic of America's "melting pot."

Since it's the middle of summer, there are no Christmas sweaters in sight. I have no clue how hot it can be in New York, so I'm overdressed. But the Hams are wearing weather-appropriate clothing: light-colored, lightweight, but kind of formal. It's just three of them: the mother, the eight-year-old daughter and the seven-year-old son. Dad is nowhere in sight. Somehow, they all look smaller, slimmer and brighter than they did in their holiday picture.

Although the kids seem fine, there's something that bothers me about the mother. She appears much more petite than she did in her photo, a bit worse for the wear. She has a pinched, witchy face and slightly demonic eyes. The smile plastered on her face looks fake. So, my earliest impression of the Hams, my moment of truth, is not the best.

Run away! a frightened voice in my head screams.
Take a deep breath and give it a chance, Maggie! another voice in my head responds.

I try to give myself a silent pep talk. *Imagine yourself in her shoes,* I tell myself. *Think how you must appear to her.*

I almost laugh out loud because I know that I don't look like my photo either. Right before I left Poland, I chopped off all my hair. To teeny-tiny Mrs. Ham, I bet I bring to mind an ax murderer, almost bald, with an inch of peach fuzz covering my scalp. A little scary, I guess.

What's next? What should I do? I ask myself. *Stay or run?*

I take a deep breath. With a wide smile, I wave at Mrs. Ham to get her attention. I remember considering yelling, 'Revenge!' but luckily, I don't. Instead, I give a long, loud, "Hiiiiiii!"

Since Mrs. Ham is very short, I lean down to give her a kiss on the cheek or at least a hug. This is how we do it back in Europe. Polish people are considered colder than the rest of our European neighbors in our traditional greeting. We kiss only once on *one* the cheek; most other European kiss at least once on *each* cheek—sometimes even three kisses on each side.

Considering that it's a first-time meeting, I swoop in for a one-cheek kiss. Mrs. Ham takes a step back, dodging my lips. She gives me a firm, businesslike handshake and a brief hug. Oops, I forgot. *This is the way it goes here,* I remind myself. *Handshakes are the norm. Rule #49.*

On autoplay in my head is one of the rules I learned just yesterday: "Limit physical contact and with confidence, look straight into the person's eyes." Shit, I tried to break a rule already and I haven't officially met my host family yet!

Taking Mrs. Ham's lead, I respond with handshakes for all three of them, even the kids. I decide to leave my first *faux pas*, my first embarrassing act, behind me. I'm sure it will be the first of many!

The drive is long enough for me to study the kids' profiles during the ride. They're both beautiful with deep, black Asian eyes. Tale, the girl, seems more responsible and more proper than her brother. Maybe because she's older by a year. The boy, Samuel, has a spark of adventure in his eyes, a mini devil always looking for trouble. I can see that he's a bundle of energy as he tries to engage me in a game. I think that's what Samuel's doing, at least. I don't totally understand him. Besides missing his front teeth, Samuel is using unfamiliar words. I just shake my head, and like Auntie Basia taught me, keep responding with, "Okay."

"He's talking about his Gameboy," Mrs. Ham explains. "It's a video game system." She catches my eye in the rearview mirror and smiles. Maybe she isn't so witchy after all.

I thank Mrs. Ham for the explanation and say to myself, *Ooof, first awkward conversation behind me.*

One highway leads to another. After about thirty minutes, we finally arrive at my home for the next year. It's in a town called Mamaroneck, which is north of Manhattan, in Westchester County. MA-MAR-O-NECK. I practice saying it in my head; it's a mouthful.

The house isn't as ginormous as I'd imagined. Just your typical, normal-sized one-family home with two cars parked in the driveway. (I figure the older-looking one is for me.) The front lawn is neat. They must have a gardener because the grass is nicely mowed and there are

Chapter Four - Family Values

plenty of flowers leading to the front door. Which Mr. Ham opens to greet us. Has he been waiting there?

Maybe it's my imagination but Mr. Ham is less enthusiastic and less warm toward me than his wife is. Maybe I'm just another Au Pair in a long line of Au Pairs. Maybe he didn't want an Au Pair at all. I will soon find out.

Everything feels well-planned, as though they've mapped it out in advance, step by step. "We'll show you the kids' rooms then we'll take you down to yours," Mrs. Ham says. Has she danced this Au Pair dance before?

Sam's room is large and disorganized with boys' toys scattered everywhere. It looks like someone tried to neaten the mess by quickly and chaotically stacking things on the shelves that line one wall. Posters of superheroes like Superman decorate the space.

Tale's room is slightly smaller but warmer, more personal, more organized. I can already tell she's the more thoughtful of the two. Lots of photos of family and friends are tacked to a cork board above her desk. Her space is super girly and painted pink.

In these quick visits, I learn where the kids' clothes are kept and how I should fold them. I also learn how to prepare them for their school day. Not only does everything have to match but everything must be perfect. I get the feeling that perfection, or at least the illusion of perfection, is important in the Ham household.

Feeling sort of off after the lecture, I hope to see my room soon. It must be big and comfy like the rest of the house. But where is it? I don't see any other rooms besides these.

Then I notice a door at the end of the hallway. *That must be it,* I tell myself. When Mrs. Ham takes me there, I learn that it's not the door to a room at all, but to a stairway. The stairs lead to the basement. That's where I find the laundry room, the kids' playroom and the garage.

It looks as if the playroom was cut in half to create another space. Welcome to my bedroom!

It's tiny with a narrow, single bed, nothing like the sumptuous beds at the hotel. There's barely enough room for anything else. Beside the bed is a little nightstand, a cabinet with a small TV on top and a medium-sized window. Nothing special. A doll's room compared to the other bedrooms. Far from being the sprawling guest room I expected, it's clearly servant's quarters. And I'm clearly their servant.

In my lowly space, there's nothing decorating the walls. Sad and stark, it immediately makes me feel depressed. Not a good feeling at the start of my stay. Maybe I've made a huge mistake. *Never mind, I can make it look better,* I cheer myself on. At least I'm separate from the whole family, though. I have my own private space down here, near the garage and a private entrance too. I can be independent, not under their constant scrutiny, which is a big deal to me.

Mrs. Ham's voice brings me back to earth. "When you unpack, come upstairs to eat. We can go over the house rules then." Crap! More rules?

"Okay," I reply with a grin on my face and mixed feelings in my heart. Auntie Basia would be proud.

•

I've only just arrived at my host home but I'm already exhausted! My head is swirling. There are so many rules to remember, so many activities the kids participate in—and that I have to take them to. I'm also expected to organize their free time and entertain them. I guess I need to learn what a Gameboy is too!

The poor Ham kids don't have much down time because as overachieving American children, they've involved in tons of activities and are expected to perform each one of them impeccably.

Chapter Four - Family Values

Before arriving in the States, nobody told me that one of my duties as an Au Pair would be playing with these kids. So, basically, not only do I have to take care of them, but I'm expected to be their "toy" too! At their age, I was playing outdoors with my friends and we didn't expect adults to entertain us. They had their own world and we had ours. But this concept is alien here. In America, kids are Number One and adults are supposed to do everything for them, even amuse them. This is the second culture shock I experience today. But what can I do?

I try to look on the positive side, though. I can always go back to Poland if I'm miserable, right? On the bright side, I have more freedom in the US than I would in Poland. I don't have a curfew and I have my own car to use any time I want. (In what little spare time I have!) I decide to accept my new reality and see what the future brings. I'll stay with the Hams, at least for the time being.

•

Driving is another challenge I face in my adopted country. In Poland, I'd gotten used to driving a standard-style car with a stick shift and clutch. Learning to master an automatic car is a totally new skill I must develop. After a few tries, I manage not to press the brake with my right foot. Though my left foot constantly seeks the clutch.

"Sit on your left leg," Mr. Ham, tells me, exasperated, almost yelling. He's getting more upset by the minute. The second day of my driver's ed, I keep looking for the stick shift. And keep forgetting to stop at the stop sign. This last one is a big no-no. There are endless full stops in Mamaroneck, one on each corner, it seems. And they come out of nowhere.

Mr. Ham doesn't appear to care what type of driver I am. Of course, he doesn't want me to kill his kids, but he seems bored giving me driving lessons. Like it's beneath him, a waste of his precious time. After all, he's an important emergency room doctor. He works long hours and probably wishes he were relaxing at home rather than watching me make same mistakes behind the wheel over and over again.

"Yes! Finally! You got it!" Mr. Ham exclaims, in shock. "Remember to keep doing it that way." Mission accomplished, he tells me, "We can go back home now. Feel free to practice more on your own." I can feel his tense body relaxing on the seat beside me.

Home. I don't know if this place will ever be home. Everything looks so strange, so different. Especially the streets. My dad used to joke that I was "born driving." I learned when I was 15 years old and always thought I was pretty good at it. Not anymore! Now, I feel like a baby starting from the beginning. Everyone drives crazy here!

For example, a guy just goes through a roundabout without putting on his signal—and doesn't even give the other cars already in the roundabout the right of way. "Oh my God!" I yell. "What the heck is he doing? He should stop and wait for me to pass! Look, there's another one trying to force their way in!"

"We don't have many traffic circles here in the US," Mr. Ham explains, amused at my outburst. With these idiots on the road, I guess I'm not the worst driver in the neighborhood.

I glance at the fuel gauge and figure I should stop at the petrol station before heading to meet my girlfriends. "How much is petrol?" I ask the guy who works at the refilling station.

"For what?" He looks at me like I'm speaking another language. Is it my accent or is he also new to the States? To my untrained eye, he looks Indian. But I can't be sure.

"P-E-T-R-O-L," I spell slowly. "How much does it cost?"

He returns my question with the same slow-motion spelling. "Do you mean G-A-S?" he wonders. Do I?

This car doesn't run on gas, does it? I didn't see any propane tanks in the trunk. This isn't just a difference in pronunciation as in the British "tomato" and the American "tomato." "Petrol" and "gas" aren't even the same words! Well, maybe they have the same meaning in the States.

"Yes! Gas!" I tell the gas boy working there, happy to solve yet another problem. He tells me not only how much it costs but gives me smile back. Feeling confident again, I drop Mr. Ham back home and take the rest of the evening off.

At school in Poland, they didn't teach us American English. It's a completely different beast than European English. What's more, no one taught me how to grow a thick outer skin for my trip to New York. (Can they even teach this?) Everyone here seems rude and a wee bit arrogant. Either way, I decide not to waste my time worrying about selfish drivers…or what to call fuel. I want meet my girls! They're waiting for me at a café in town.

The town of Mamaroneck is about 40 minutes north of Manhattan. The main attraction is the local Starbucks. All the nearby Au Pairs are meeting here to share their babysitting experiences, including challenges with their host families. It's fun to hear what others are going through, especially since their encounters mirror mine. Some of my colleagues say they go down to New York City for weekends visits. I haven't been there yet but am dying to.

•

Fast forward two months. This is when I finally make it to the city. It's only 25 miles from Mamaroneck to Manhattan but it seems hundreds. It's almost eight weeks before I can make the pilgrimage down on Metro-North because I'm so busy with the Ham kids and adjusting to my new life. But today is the day!

The railroad conductor says the trip will take less than an hour. Plenty of time to sit back, relax and reflect on the past two months. It all went by so fast, filled with everyday routines and enjoyable meetups with my Au Pair girls. My typical day starts at 7 a.m., which is when I wake up Tale and Samuel. Sometimes they're already awake, which makes it easier. While they get ready for school, I fix their lunch boxes then drop them off at the local public school. It's close to home and convenient. Mid-afternoon, I pick them up again.

So, from around 9 a.m. to around 2 p.m., I have a few hours to myself. Although I can't go far, in case there's a problem. If they get sick, for example, in which case, I'd have to get them early, of course. Post-pickup hours are filled with after-school sports, homework and dinner. When Mr. and Mrs. Ham come home from work, I'm off the rest of the evening. Phew!

Sunday is my day off which I start looking forward to on Monday. I call it "Maggie Time." But Monday through Saturday, everything is extremely organized and rigorously scheduled. There's no room for mistakes, just like in the bank my host mom works for.

It takes an enormous effort for me to follow through with all my duties. As you might have already guessed, I'm not a "by the book" sort of person. I have strong doubts about being able to manage this tight schedule for a whole year. My one saving grace is my girls. Meeting with the other Au Pairs helps me survive.

We get together almost every Sunday. We explore the area and those of us over 21 hang out in local bars. This is another culture shock for us: the drinking age in the US. Throughout most of the world, the legal drinking age is 18, but not here in America. Like most of my European counterparts, I remember drinking wine or vodka with my parents on family occasions since I was 15 and going

Chapter Four - Family Values

to bars at the age of 17. Because of the drinking age in America, not all the Au Pairs can meet at a bar, so Starbucks becomes our hangout spot.

Out of all the babysitters, I only deeply connect with two. The first is Joys, the Brazilian girl I shared my hotel room with, and the second is Hannah, a sweet girl from Germany. Joys is a wild, spontaneous, emotional young woman, while Hannah, who is tall with blue eyes and long blonde hair, is calm and pragmatic. It's an interesting combo platter that makes us the perfect trio. We balance each other out nicely. Because their English is much better than mine, sometimes I have trouble keeping up with the conversation but they're patient with me. In many ways, they enrich my Au Pair life. And help keep me sane.

The conductor's voice announces that we're approaching the final station, the world-famous Grand Station Terminal. I've heard so much about it. Grand Central is one of the oldest and most architecturally-beautiful buildings in New York City. It serves both as a long-distance train station and a local subway station. It has popular dining spots and underground shops. There's even an old oyster bar which I'm sure I could never afford. Indeed, Grand Central doesn't disappoint.

My head spins as I take in the high, arched ceiling studded with constellations and zodiac signs. The deep turquoise looks like it's painted in a mirror that reflects backwards. The tall, sloped windows at one end let in ribbons of natural light. My surroundings glow gold. Amazed by the grandeur, I almost forget that I'm supposed to meet my date beneath the celebrated Grand Central Terminal clock. Apparently, the clock gives the most correct time in the city, and it's said that New Yorkers set their watches by it. The clock is gorgeous—four-sided, polished brass and it sits on top of the information booth.

Almost 11 o'clock, I still have a few minutes before my date arrives. I figure I should fix myself up before meeting him and search for a bathroom. I'm excited about meeting Paul my first time in Manhattan and want to make a good impression on him. I find a restroom downstairs and end up in a long line that moves quickly. People in the station itself look like they're taking part in competition, chasing each other into the unknown on what should be a slow, lazy Sunday morning. I can only imagine how fast the pace is on a workday.

Even the pace on the ladies' room line is rushed, orchestrated by a bathroom attendant with a seriously mean expression on her face. She must be extremely unhappy to work on a weekend, and it shows. I feel sorry for her and give her a smile. But she only responds with an aggressive "Next!" and points to the left. I'm disappointed that the restroom isn't full of gorgeous murals on the walls and ceiling like the rest of Grand Central is but go about my business as quickly as possible.

By the time I get back upstairs to the clock, Paul is waiting for me. He's even more handsome than I remember, tall, dark-haired, with light brown skin. The sun, as it pours in through the gigantic windows of the main hall, reflects on his face, making him even more attractive. It sharpens his gorgeous bone structure and makes his chestnut eyes sparkle. I hope the sunlight makes me look equally as attractive to him.

Paul is Peruvian. We met in a bar one night in Mamaroneck where he was hanging out with his friends. He's about to take me on one of the best dates in my life because it's in New York City. My first time! We haven't even kissed yet but I'm hoping it will happen today—on my romantic New York City date.

Paul smiles at me and grabs my hand, "Let's go!'" he says. We run fast down the stairs to catch a train. "On the weekend, they only run every half hour," he explains. I follow my tour guide/date and hop onto a subway car.

As the doors close behind us, I'm squeezed between two people. I can barely see Paul because he's pushed

Chapter Four - Family Values

practically to the other end of the train car. I feel slightly panicky, like I can't breathe, but I'm still happy we made the train. Or am I?

Wait a minute, I don't even know where we're going. Paul mentions a big surprise, that he's taking me to a very popular spot, but where and what it is, I have no idea. What if he's a serial killer? Will he take me to Central Park, to ride on the famous carousel, then drag me into the woods to rape and murder me? Suddenly I'm terrified. I only met Paul a couple of times. Why do I trust him so easily? I know almost nothing about him. Oh, naïve Maggie!

But Paul is very polite, I remind myself. (I bet Jeffrey Dahmer was polite too!) Paul has trustful eyes, I tell myself. Hey, wait, isn't New York City known as one of the most dangerous places on earth? All those creepy movies from the 1970s pop into my head...*Death Wish, The French Connection.* There are probably still a lot of crazy people lurking in these crowds. Paul could be one of them.

Take a deep breath Maggie! I tell myself. Either way it's too late to do anything now. And it's 2002, not 1974. Plus, I have a cell phone. I can always use it to call 911 in case of an emergency, as I learned at my Au Pair orientation. The thought alone calms me. I decide to still go for it. At least I'll ride the Central Park merry-go-round before I die, right?

Although I send Paul a bright smile across the subway car, all I get is a worried look in return. He's focused on listening to the garbled announcements coming over the loudspeaker. I hear something about the train being rerouted but am not sure what that means. It says we need to catch a shuttle bus at the next station.

"We've been on the train almost an hour," I tell Paul, exasperated. "How long will it take us to finally get to our destination?"

"I don't know," he admits. "I think we should jump on another train instead."

"Okay," I tell him. "You're my guide. Either way, I don't know where I'm going."

"I'm taking you to a nice place, just trust me," Paul says. I try to trust him but…

After more than two hours, Paul discovers that there is no way we can get to the Bronx Zoo on the train today. "The Bronx Zoo?" I sigh. "I'm allergic to most of the animals there." He's disappointed, especially when I admit to him, "I'm tired. Can you please just take me back to Grand Central?"

Paul shakes his head, defeated, his plans for a special day ruined by the MTA. In silence, we take the train back toward midtown, which takes another two hours. He drops me off at Grand Central Terminal. I'm all alone.

This is without a doubt the worst date in my life. But it was so promising! I imagined tons of laughs, alcohol, city lights and a party atmosphere, at least in my dream. Instead, it was more like a nightmare, shuttling back and forth underground on the crowded, dirty subway. I imagined my date would be a "Sex and the City" episode. But it was far from it!

Looking back, I'm not sure if I was ever really interested in Paul—or guys in general. To me, Paul represented the key to the city: a hot, hunky tour guide who knew his way around Manhattan. But that turned out not to be the case.

Just so the day isn't a total loss, I decide to at least take a walk through the streets around Grand Central to see some of the Promised Land. I push open a heavy bronze and glass door. There I am, standing in the middle of 42nd Street, surrounded by the tallest buildings I've ever seen in my life. Skyscrapers are everywhere and they're so tall I can barely see the sky. It's astonishing but also cold and scary. I have this overwhelming feeling that the

Chapter Four - Family Values

buildings are pressing me to the ground, that they're a heavy load on my back. Paralyzing me.

When I look up 42nd Street, the buildings and sidewalks seem to merge into one big concrete, steel and glass jungle. I struggle to get my breathing back to normal. I'm trying to take it slowly but that's impossible in the speeding wave of people that spring at me from every direction. The way they move looks disorganized, but it actually has a silent, secret rhythm. It reminds me of the way water in a river follows the same current.

When a body goes against the grain and swerves into another person, there's a loud "Fuck off!" These outbursts immediately regulate traffic. I quickly adjust to the flow of the streets. Although I'm overwhelmed by the city, I kind of love it here. I'm pushed by an invisible energy. It's so vibrant, active and alive! I want to be part of it! I think.

A group of people catch my eye. They're surrounding an object, staring down at it. Something important must be happening. I go check it out. When I get closer, I see police officers standing between the crowd and what resembles a large bean bag on the ground. What is it? What's happening?

Even nearer now, I see that it's not a bag at all, but a body on the ground. Behind me, a woman's voice rings out, "He's already dead! He jumped out the window. He just committed suicide." Poor guy!

Welcome to the Big Apple, Maggie…

I can't wait to get back to the safety of the suburbs.

Chapter Five
Professional Sitter

A year has passed since my arrival in the US. My excitement about the Au Pair job turned out to be more than its reality. The first few months, I was still exploring and learning. I tried to visit New York City (and other nearby cities on the East Coast) as much as I could. I also made a trip to visit family in California for Christmas and went to Arizona and Utah. All these extracurricular activities wouldn't be possible without having extra income on the side.

Being an Au Pair only provides pocket money. Back in Poland, $160 a month goes far but not in the US. It's barely enough for necessities. The host family provides a bit more cash, only it's still not enough for us. However, it's a bargain for the host family. The cost of hiring a live-in helper like an Au Pair is a hell of a lot less than hiring a regular babysitter part-time. Plus, they get round-the-clock help.

Besides our weekly wages, the host family pays for the Au Pair's food, our flights to and from the US and English classes. But we still have to pay for necessities like personal hygiene items (deodorant, tampons…), train tickets to the city and Starbucks coffees when we meet our friends for our weekly "mental health" sessions.

Back in Poland, I had no clue how little our stipend was by US standards. But I learn it that first week in Mamaroneck when I spend a month's wages one night out in a bar. That's when I decide to look for another babysitting job on the side. With the help of a friend who does the same thing, I find two other families who call me for weekend babysitting gigs. It's steady money and I am determined to save it.

The kids are almost the same age as Tale and Samuel. I already feel more comfortable in my childcare role and with my English-language skills. I spend a year with babysitting as my side hustle. So, by the time my Au Pair stint is over, I've managed to save a small nest egg. Not only do I have more experience, but I've built up a professional network. Only do I want to babysit my whole life? I have some hard questions to answer.

After much thought, I decide to return to Poland to finish college—not only is school more expensive in the States but I my English isn't strong enough to complete my studies in that language. So, I go back home to Poland.

After graduation, I decide to return to the States, where my girlfriend Iwona is waiting for me. (We'd met in the Au Pair Program.) In Brooklyn, to be exact. I want to give my American Dream one more shot. And if I fail again, I figure I can always go back to Europe. But love is a deciding factor in my choice to go back to the US.

As hard as I try, I can't find work in my new field, which is international relations. I have no choice but to apply for a full-time babysitting job. To be honest, I don't like the work, but the work likes me. Plus, I'm good at it. So, babysitter becomes my profession by default. I figure it's my only possibility to make money in New York if I want to stay here. Which I do. Maybe I can even save enough money to invest in my future. I can start learning a skill that will put me onto a new career path. But to do that, I need to get another babysitting gig. And fast.

My efforts pay off quickly. I get an interview right out of the gate, after only one day of searching. A family with two elementary school kids is looking for a full-time sitter. And the salary isn't bad. I take the train from deep Brooklyn to the upper East Side of Manhattan.

There's a saying that people from Brooklyn never go higher than Union Square. But this time, I'm venturing way above 14th Street. It takes over an hour to get there. During the subway ride, I give a quick glance at my beefed-up resume and go over answers to questions I might get asked during the interview. I'm ready to kill it!

Relieved that the long ride hasn't killed me beforehand, I finally arrive at the East 86th Street subway station on the Lexington Avenue IRT line. I immediately take a shine to this quiet, fancy residential part of the city. The Metropolitan Museum of Art and Central Park add to the allure. It's far from where I'm crashing in Brooklyn but I'm willing to give the job a try.

After checking my reflection in my cellphone's black screen, I ring the doorbell. I'm immediately astonished by the size of the apartment. I guess it's typical for the Upper East Side but it's jaw-dropping for me. The building itself was probably built in the mid-19th century and boasts huge rooms and extremely high ceilings. It must take a ton of work for the housekeeper to keep this castle clean. And not just because the apartment is so humongous but because the Stevens Family are slobs!

Stuff is literally thrown everywhere: clothes, towels, toys and dirty dishes. Seated on top of one of the clothes mountains is a small child, maybe five years old. Another child of about three is staring at the TV. He must be watching something fascinating because he doesn't even acknowledge me.

The third child is only a couple of months old. I notice the baby immediately because it's in its mother's arms when she opens the door and invites me inside. Mom looks messy herself and is slightly arrogant. She doesn't exactly say hello. Instead, her greeting is, "Come inside! This is my house!" It's as if her home is the most important thing about her. The woman's lack of a proper greeting sends the silent message that she thinks she's better than me and that she's the boss here. By working for the rich, I've become skilled at reading between the lines.

I don't know why Mrs. Stevens is mean to me right off the bat. Is it because of my Eastern European accent? Or is it because I'm *just a babysitter*? Or maybe she sees me as a potential predator who could seduce her husband in the very near future. I'm definitely more attractive than she is. And younger.

Who knows what's going on in her pointy, little head, right? Maybe it's just a touch of post-partum depression. But whatever it is, everything is weird from the beginning. The whole feel of the Stevens household isn't good. I don't see anything positive coming from being there. But I stay for the interview, even against my better judgement.

"You basically need to take care of the two older kids," Mrs. Stevens explains. "Sometimes I'll ask you to help me with the baby but mostly he's with me. I take care of him. Oh, and there's light housekeeping involved." Light housekeeping! The place is a wreck!

"I have experience with preschool and elementary school kids," I assure Mrs. Stevens. "But what exactly is light housekeeping? What does it involve?"

"Oh, it's just laundry, dusting and vacuuming. And cleaning bathrooms, too," she adds. *Just?* I ask myself. *Just?* This sounds like heavy housekeeping. But I keep my cool. "And how much extra does the cleaning job pay?"

Mrs. Stevens looks shocked. "Why, it's included. It's a part of the babysitting job. The kids make such a mess and most of the laundry is theirs anyway." She stares me down, as if daring me to respond. I'm shocked that she expects full housekeeping service without paying extra for it. At first, I think she's joking. But she isn't.

I try to mirror Mrs. Stevens's arrogance in my voice. "You're kidding, right? A cleaning-lady job is another full-time position. And you just pay just 15 dollars an hour?" I'm surprised by my aggressive response. So is she. But I just can't take it anymore, feeling like a slave. "That's not going to work!" I tag on.

Mrs. Stevens looks pissed off at my cocky attitude, but she still tries to keep me from leaving. As I'm gathering my things, she adds excuses about the payment and the position. But by that point, I'm not listening anymore. All I'm thinking about is how I can get out of there quickly and safely, without this crazy, sloppy woman bashing in my head.

I go out on a few other interviews but they're not successful either. Either the money is bad or the family is nuts and has bizarre rules or they have too many expectations. I'm getting tired of it. The whole babysitting thing is not working out. My American Dream of starting from nothing and climbing the stairway of success isn't materializing, no matter how hard I try.

But wait, isn't this how the America Dream should look? Many tries, many failures and finally, success. I remind myself that New York City is full of opportunities but only if you work hard. Then you'll get somewhere.

But another part of me—that small, scared part— tries to convince Hopeful Maggie that the concept is bullshit. Connections and luck seem to be what really gets you far in America, not drive and determination. I'm downhearted until I get a call from Anna, another Au Pair.

After the Au Pair program ended, Anna decided to stay in the US and managed to hook up with a wealthy family. She arranges for me to speak with her boss about a position that's just opened up. It sounds promising but I try not to get my hopes up.

During the phone call the following day, Anna introduces me to Mrs. Willis, her employer. The Willis Family has two older girls and one boy. Plus, an army of housekeepers and one babysitter (Anna). They're looking for extra help at their summer house in East Hampton. Because I'm highly recommended by Anna, the job is mine if I want it. Without a face-to-face interview. I'm pleasantly surprised.

"Maggie, we've heard so much about you from Anna that we already love you," Mrs. Willis says. "Just come to the Hamptons this weekend. We have two dogs that need to be taken care of. Oh, and if you need extra money, we can hire you on as a housekeeper to stay with us for the season."

Mr. Willis explains, "Our other housekeepers can only come in twice a week and that's not enough. Of course, we'll pay you more for cleaning if you decide to stay with us." What? They're not expecting me to walk the dogs AND clean the house for only $15 an hour? Outrageous!

Mrs. Willis, who insists I call her "Ruth," sounds nice, super friendly. I can feel her warm smile over the phone. Everything is so promising, almost too good to be true. And I get to take care of dogs instead of kids. "Okay, I'll come Friday night and stay until Sunday evening if that's all right," I answer.

"That's great," Mrs. Willis tells me. She gives me the address and thanks me...actually thanks me for coming out to the Hamptons for a trial run.

I hang up the phone and start jumping up and down, screaming. "Yes!" I can't believe I just got a job working in New York's most exclusive beach community, the Hamptons. This is where Manhattan's uber-wealthy spend their summers. And my job is to take care of dogs. I love dogs! Is this even real?

To get to know them, I spend the weekend with the Willis Family and their pups. Right away, they love me and vice versa. One dog is a cute, old Jack Russell terrier and the other is a young, energetic white Labrador retriever. I play with the dogs and have wonderful time. At the end of the weekend, Ruth asks, "So how do you like it here?" What? She really cares about what I think?!

Ruth continues, "We like you a lot and it looks like the dogs do too. So, how about it? Would you like to work the whole summer for us in the Hamptons?"

"Yes, I would!" I can hardly contain my excitement. The Willis gig offers a decent salary plus pleasant accommodations. I share an entire wing of the beach house with my friend Anna, who works as their babysitter. The dogs bunk with us most of time. I feed them, walk them and wash them after long swims, which they love. The house faces the ocean and there's a nearby lake where the dogs enjoy swimming.

Anna and I are given the use of a new SUV so we can be more independent. There's no public transportation in the Hamptons so driving is the only way to get around. And we have a new car, at that. It's awesome. I couldn't ask for more my second year in the US. Taking on the job of dog "nanny" is ideal. Even cleaning the house, my side hustle, is easier than I thought it would be. (The Willis Family aren't pigs like the Stevens family was!)

Sunday, my day off, is mostly a beach day. I also spend it visiting local restaurants with Anna. The Hamptons vibe is pretty mellow and time passes quickly. Before I know it, Labor Day is here, which means the end of the season is upon us.

I'm happy to have made some money to save for college and spent time on a gorgeous beach in the Hamptons. But life on Long Island is slow-paced and lazy. I'll be glad to get back to the city; I miss it. And I don't need to worry about my next job because Ruth says I can stay with them after the summer is over. Again, I say, "Yes!"

The Willis home is just outside the city, in Westchester. It's a striking castle of a house with views of the Hudson River. Again, I have a separate room in a private corner of the house. It's much nicer than my tiny quarters off the garage in the Hams' home. I think I'll like it here.

On the surface, it's the American Dream. But behind the pretty picture is another reality. An ugly one.

For one thing, the Willis Family is completely out of balance. Whatever they do is for show. Although they're generous with their staff, material wealth is the most important thing to them. Ruth and her husband Jim fight with each other nonstop. The whole house can hear their raging arguments. Ruth doesn't work and gets totally immersed in social activities and the eBay shoppers' community. She spends tons of money buying expensive designer handbags. All day long, she's locked in her gigantic closet, glued to her computer, searching for the perfect bag. I don't think she'll ever find it.

Jim works all the time. He's in the banking industry and has tons of meetings (and God knows what else!) that fill up his day. Mostly, he's out of the house. And when he's home, he and Ruth argue. They fight over countless things: money, his escort girls and whatever else comes their way. The entire household is on edge. Especially the kids.

Mina, the younger girl, has issues a wealthy twelve-year-old shouldn't have. Her emotional problems have manifested in the form of an eating disorder. My friend Anna's job is to control Mina's habit of overeating. Anna literally must guard Mina to make sure she stays away from the fridge.

Holly, the sixteen-year-old, is much easier to look after. Anna just has to drive her to after-school activities and other social events. It's clear that Holly is also tired of the house dynamics. She's at the age when everything is an "Oh my God!" situation. She's curious about life, still exploring people and things to find out where she fits into

Chapter Five - Professional Sitter

the world. Understandably, Holly tries to stay away from home as much as she can.

Rounding out the family is Scott, a twenty-two-year-old who's away at college. We don't see Scott much, and I know why.

The home environment isn't healthy. Although the pay is good, Anna and I are getting tired of the toxic atmosphere and the general craziness we're exposed to every day. It's especially stressful for Anna. I committed to only one more season after the summer, so I need to start looking for another job. By now the excitement of working at the East Hampton beach house is gone. This isn't how I imagined my American Dream in the United States. After all, I have a master's degree in international relations. I'm not a dogsitter or a housekeeper!

I spend hours crying and start to give up hope. It doesn't make sense to stay in the States, wasting my time on menial jobs. I don't see a future for me here, at least not as a babysitter or a housekeeper. I'm no one in the US.

I admit that my situation isn't as bad as an immigrant who escapes from an oppressive regime and crosses the border illegally. I didn't have to spend time in a detention room, forever waiting for my case to be resolved, only to get deported in the end. I'm definitely in a better situation than other refugees. However, I still need to start from zero to reach my American Dream. So far, my quest has gotten me nowhere.

I apply to jobs at the United Nations that would utilize my educational background. But having no connections and no solid work experience in my field, it doesn't lead anywhere. So, I'm stuck in the Babysitting and Housekeeping Department. Those are the only things I can do. Maybe I'll try my luck in a more normal household. But for now, I do a little and dream big.

Since I'm an expert cleaning lady and babysitter, I decide to look for employment in these two professions. Among my offers is one that looks attractive and combines both housekeeping and childcare. I set up an interview in Brooklyn Heights. It's become my favorite neighborhood with its beautiful brownstones, stately row houses and lovely churches. Brooklyn Heights is a landmarked historic district with a promenade that has an amazing view of Lower Manhattan's skyscrapers. It's refreshingly multicultural with Lebanese Christians and Caribbeans living there. Other ethnic groups like Italians and Latinos are sprinkled in. Brooklyn Heights used to be a gay neighborhood but in recent years, became inhabited by professionals like lawyers and doctor. It's family oriented with lots of parks.

In this case, the location determines my choice. I often hang out in Brooklyn Heights with friends and love it there. But now, I'm in Brooklyn Heights for work. After a short telephone interview, I go for an in-person meetup, which is pretty much just a formality. Francie Jacoby shows me around the three-story house and goes over my responsibilities. Her home is stunning and my duties sound simple. I start the next day.

The vacuum cleaner and a jug of bleach become my best friends. Each day, I focus on cleaning a different part of the house. Besides cleaning, I drive Francie's son Ron to school and around town when school is out. He's 16 years old and will soon have his own driver's license but until then, I'm his chauffeur. Ron goes to an exclusive private school nearby. He's bright and on the surface, seems to be doing well. But in his private life, Ron has many personal issues—like controlling his temper. When he's angry or doesn't get his way, Ron destroys things around the house. And I have to clean up after his rage.

For the most part, Ron keeps his distance from me. We barely talk. Ron's dad is very old and wheelchair ridden. Francie much younger than her husband, in her early fifties. She's so calm and polite. Most of the time, Francie also keeps her distance, but this gives me a wide berth to do my own thing. I come to the Jacoby household early each morning to make breakfast for Mr. J, take Ron to school, clean up and drive Ron back home after school. Since I'm the only housekeeper, I devise a cleaning schedule to my advantage. I go on breaks often and take naps in the basement playroom. In the afternoon, a Filipino woman comes to cook dinner. Violetta and I always chat before I go home. Sometimes, this is the only conversation I've had the whole day.

"You've been working here a few months," Francie starts one winter day. In my head, I think, *Yeah, work and nap.* Is Francie going to give me a bonus? The holiday season is right around the corner; extra money would be welcome. "We really like you but...," Francie continues. Uh-oh, here it comes! "...but we don't feel this job is right for you. You're too intelligent. Maybe you should find something that's a better fit." Francie adds.

I think, *Yeah, it's not as if I haven't tried!* I bite my tongue and say nothing. Instead of a response, I just give her a forced smile and respond, "You're right. Maybe it's time for me to move on."

I can't believe Francie is firing me right now! She has no idea how much I would love to work in my profession or find a new career path. But so far, my search has led me nowhere. And I've just hit another dead end.

Chapter Six

Serving is Fun!

"Remember, serve from the right and clean from the left!" Or did my boss say just the opposite: "Serve from left....?" Who knew bringing people food could be so complicated.

I hesitate while putting the plate on the table in front of my customer. My boss's words ring in my ears but I get confused again. It must be the stress of serving a table of 12 that's messing with my head. I'm working a prominent New York City charity event with at least 200 in attendance, and I'm responsible for feeding a dozen of them.

All the guests look so elegant. There are long dresses, tuxedos, lots of expensive-smelling perfumes, speechifying and excellent music. I love the atmosphere but serving so many fancy people at once makes me stressed. *I didn't mix it up this time. It's from left to right,* I assure myself.

My table is all served and satisfied. I pour more wine from the right. It's hard to squeeze between the guests, who sit on high, heavy chairs. It's tough to reach the wine glasses, which seem so far away on the table. I try to pour without spilling a drop. As they talk, people move around and wave their hands. It's like pouring wine in an obstacle course! I'm afraid I'll trip over the long dresses, purses and other items that litter the floor. Serving is a real challenge. As I perform my duties, I'm required to smiling. All the time. My face feels like it's going to crack.

I'm worried because I really need to crush at this gig. My first time serving, I can't afford to lose this job. After Francie unceremoniously fired me, my Polish friend Monika recommends me for work as a server. Thankfully, I'm not a housekeeper anymore. As challenging as my new line of work can be, I enjoy the whole jumbled mishmash of the catering business. It's fast-paced and hectic and always different. Plus, it's the holiday season in New York City so fundraisers and corporate events abound. I love parties, loud parties, and people.

Sometimes I wish I could be on the other side of the equation: having a blast and being served. But that's not possible, not yet. I'm a server and this is what I do now. I don't want to repeat my last few years as a babysitter/housekeeper. But I need money and decide to give the service industry a go. I'll try to cull as much as I can from it. I'll observe and learn about the catering business, which has sparked my interest. I even apply to take a course in Tourism and Hospitality at a local CUNY college. (CUNY stands for "City University of New York," by the way.) I want to learn more about hospitality and customer service, something I think I'd be good at.

So ultimately, Francie does me a favor by firing me. Because by firing me, she forces me to look for something new and it's brought me here. Besides, I'm enjoying my job at this posh midtown hotel. I love the music and the menu. Yes, we get to eat here too, but after everyone else has eaten. The grub is ridiculously delicious; they hire excellent chefs.

I like the people I work with. Most of them are Polish but there are some Brazilians, Russians and Canadians thrown in for good measure. It's a rich tapestry. Most of

Chapter Six - Serving is Fun!

them are actors earning extra money on the side, trying to survive. New York City is expensive! All of us have fun together, despite the pressure of urban life. And then there's the free alcohol.

Taking secret sips of rum behind the bar helps my first-day jitters. My table's already been served coffee and dessert, and everyone is up on the dance floor. A little tipsy, I feel the music's vibes and my legs start moving of their own accord. I get lost in space and time. In trance. Out of nowhere, a voice behind me barks, "Stop dancing and get more water for your table!" This drags me back to earth.

I'm only gone a few seconds, but it feels like an eternity. I was lost in the moment when my boss brings me back to reality—and the dining room. He catches me daydreaming and dancing as he scans the room, checking on each table. I'm still learning how to avoid him and hide undetected with a stolen appetizer or snack. This is the first time I've been caught—so far.

Just as I'm getting the hang of my new job, the event ends. The music slows down and people begin leaving. I look at my watch and can't believe that it's only 11 p.m.

I guess I'm used to the European (read that as Polish) style of parting where the festivities don't start until after midnight and continue until dawn. With a huge hangover to show for it the next day! In the US, everything is well orchestrated and paid for in advance. Plus, parties end on time. It's almost as if there was no party at all. *Good for me,* I think. *I can finish early and go home.* No complaints because I'm tired from being on my feet all night.

During the busy season, I have three to four parties a week. Most of them take place in hotels, the United Nation building, embassies or well-known restaurants. Sometimes they're in sumptuous apartments, fancy bars or outdoor, heated tents. New York is known as the city that never sleeps and it's true. There are big, splashy gatherings for absolutely everything—Halloween,

Thanksgiving, the New York City Marathon, birthdays, bat and bar mitzvah, weddings and any other celebration you can imagine. The attendees are diverse, ranging from young, wild hipsters, old snobs, the filthy rich, religious Jews and crazy long-distance runners. The whole Manhattan crazy quilt is in attendance. Some parties are loud and others, quite tame. Some are filled with government officials and otherwise elegant souls while others are populated with a more down-to-earth clientele. Some guests are kind while others are rude and act entitled.

One party in particular comes to mind: Halloween at Tavern on the Green. It's a trendy, iconic restaurant, popular especially with out-of-towners. Located in the middle of Central Park's Sheep Meadow, it's well-known not only for its prime location but for its over-the-top decor. It was built in 1870 and serves the local elite, artists, writers, governors and even presidents. The striking brick building is filled with a slew of smaller dining rooms. Hideously abundant in red, green and blue carpets, there are too many details crammed into the space, including heavy crystal chandeliers. To me, it's a crazy hodgepodge.

I circle from one dining room to another, feeling like Alice in Wonderland. In the center of the restaurant is a glass-encased room overlooking the restaurant garden. Supposedly, it has an 800-person seating capacity. The place is large but not necessarily safe because of all the convoluted dining rooms that sprout one from the other. I can't imagine the chaos if a fire ever broke out, especially during one of their overblown, drunken events. Each year Tavern on the Green hosts Halloween and New Year Eve parties besides other events, including New York City Marathon parties.

But this particular Halloween is the worst party I've experienced since I started working as a server. Everyone with a paid ticket can get in but others without tickets are

Chapter Six - Serving is Fun!

trying to bribe their way inside. Most of them are loud, tipsy, young fellows with money. They're seeking alcohol, sex and adventure. They're arrogant, break all the rules of civility, scream and jump up on tables. Frankly, it scares me.

The place is extremely crowded and in order to serve my customers, I need to squeeze by with a full tray of appetizers. They descend upon me like vultures. My tray is empty within seconds. I keep refilling it constantly, taking many trips back to the kitchen. I keep my tray high, above the heads of the crowd, but I'm always getting jostled.

During one of my kitchen rounds, I feel something hot on my back. I turn and see a guy with a cigarette, his hand halfway down my back. He laughs and in a drunken voice slurs, "I hope you're not mad." I smell the stench of smoldering fabric. That asshole just burned a hole in my new jacket!

I'm about to explode when a friend passes with an empty tray. He immediately sees what's happening and gets between me and the drunk. My savior smiles and tells the guy, "Dude, you're not allowed to smoke in here. But if you put your cigarette out, I'll bring you another beer."

I can't tolerate rich, entitled idiots. In a flash, I'm ready to quit. *This is not what my American Dream looks like,* I think. I turn and stomp to the kitchen.

For these occasions, we're hired to help the regular staff. Large events are different than typical restaurant work. My colleagues and I are well trained in navigating the waters of these complex affairs. We provide skills like professional table service, passing food, bartending, set up and control the flow of bodies.

We're also taught to follow cultural mores at special events that take place in Arabic embassies, for example. One cultural rule is that women serve women and that serving is from the right hand, not the "dirty left hand," which is used for personal hygiene—like wiping your bottom. It's customary to pour coffee using a special pot called a *dallah* in the left hand while keeping the cups in your right hand. The respect and attention you give guests during the traditional coffee ceremony is highly valued. In many cases, only a male server can perform the *dallah* coffee service.

Our staff is also trained in the proper way to present Arabic cuisine. One of the rules is that there must be a mass of grub mounded onto every platter. The sheer amount of food is part of the presentation. Looking chintzy is frowned upon. The offerings must be copious and piled up like a hill, plus be pleasing to the eye. The more you load onto a plate, the better. At these jobs, we also do set up, serve and help with kitchen prep.

Most of their Arabic parties are family style, which means that giant platters line the tables so guests can help themselves. Other times, the staff circles the table with heaping plates of food, each of us carrying a different item, plating up the guests one by one. The serving preference all depends on the party.

I love this sort of gathering—full of fragrant Arabic cuisine, lively music and no alcohol. (No alcohol equals no drunks.) For the Christian soirees, there's alcohol but religious Christians tend not to get too wasted. They're less formal than the Muslim gatherings, and our staff is more involved in kitchen prep. The atmosphere is more laid back and friendly.

United Nation events are a totally unique, however. As you can imagine, they are super organized and upscale. Most of the UN parties are to celebrate an international event, day or an important dignitary's visit. There are also "culture day" parties, which I like the best. They're brimming with guests from all over the world dressed in traditional costumes where traditional dishes are served. There's often ethnic music and folkloric dance shows. These are the most relaxing and enjoyable events to work. They're the total opposite of the stiff, formal gathering where not even the tiniest *faux pas* is permitted when passing around food or serving dignities at the table. Service must be stellar.

The staff works hard and pays attention to detail to get the job done expertly. Most of the UN events entail a five-to-eight-hour workday, including prepping, serving and cleaning up. But sometimes events are even longer, often extending into the next day. This happens every year on New York City Marathon Day.

The evening prior to the marathon, Tavern on The Green hosts VIPs and serves a hot meal, buffet-style. The setup is intimate with several dining rooms featuring a variety of foodstuffs and warm, seasonal drinks. Servers at each station make sure the lines move smoothly. You can feel the excitement in the air for Marathon Day. No one can stop talking about the race and no one wants to leave. This event always lasts until the wee hours.

The day of the marathon we start serving breakfast early. So early, it doesn't make sense to go home. Most of us either sleep curled up in chairs or never end up going to bed.

Marathon Day itself is exhausting—and not just for the runners. Besides the early-bird breakfast, we serve lunch to the runners who end up at Central Park. The smell of good chow and the runners' sweat mingle, creating an interesting aroma. Their exhaustion—and ours—invades the space. Yes, the runners are tired from doing 26 miles but the servers have worked the past 24-hours with few breaks. I feel united with the marathoners in pain but not enthusiasm. I want this to be over soon.

On Thanksgiving Day, we work at the Museum of Arts and Design. I'm impressed with this place, perched in the middle of Columbus Circle with sweeping views of Central Park. Fall is especially spectacular, the park painted in red and gold just beyond the museum's windows.

The MAD building itself is nicely decorated too. Each floor is meant to be a museum in and of itself. There's an entire floor dedicated to parties. The interior decorations change at MAD constantly, always matching the décor of the exhibits. It's light, modern, a little twisted and specific in color and design.

I like working at MAD, especially the Thanksgiving party, which pays double because it's a holiday. The only thing I don't like is the mean kitchen crew and the crazy female chef. Oh, and the fact that there's no elevator the staff can use to bring food from the ninth-floor kitchen to the seventh-floor party room. So, we use the stairs to run plates two floors down. In a building that pays homage to art and design, I can't help but wonder who designed this horrible setup. The servers' comfort and safety obviously were never considered.

The Thanksgiving party at MAD is another long day because we serve breakfast AND lunch. People pay top dollar to eat breakfast with the best view of Macy's Thanksgiving Day parade from seven floors up. I wake at 5 a.m. to be there at 6 a.m. We set up breakfast, which starts around eight, first making strong coffee to perk us up. It's usually just five servers sleepily setting up a buffet table with rolls, muffins, bagels, jams and cream cheese. There's also a beverage table with coffee, tea and cold drinks. Breakfast is only for 10 or 15 guests and we don't have any food or drinks to pass around. We keep busy bussing tables and replenishing the buffet. This slow, relaxed pace gives the servers an opportunity to enjoy the parade as well.

The view from the seventh floor is tremendous. Before the parade begins, we get to watch the crowd slowly fill the streets. This starts early in the morning. By the time the staff arrives at six, there are already people from all over the world who've been on the street since the night before. Come morning, they roll up their sleeping bags and have hot coffee at Columbus Circle, happy to have

Chapter Six - Serving is Fun!

held a good spot to watch the parade overnight. They're pretty cheerful for people who have slept on the concrete.

By 7 a.m. more people arrive with folding chairs and breakfast. By nine, those fully awake, showered and shaved make an appearance. They still hope to get a place in the front. You can see the disappointment on their faces when they realize that the early birds have nabbed the best spots.

After several hours, the frozen crowd starts moving and waving. The parade has begun! The waitstaff gathers at the windows. We smile at each other, feeling like VIPs ourselves, knowing we have the best viewing area of all. We get to watch the parade from a cozy vantage point—and get paid for it.

•

Christmas is just around the corner. Early in the season, I already have four Christmas parties booked in various venues around the city, including Grand Central Station, office buildings and private apartments. They all look the same with Christmas trees, seasonal dishes and, of course, have the same stale Christmas music blaring. The only things that change are the people and their behavior.

Guests at the corporate gatherings are mostly young, ambitious individuals who sport phony smiles. Their talk is all about work, current projects and opportunities for recognition. At parties in private apartments there's a slightly warmer, family vibe but everyone seems to be a showoff. The talk centers around their kids' educations, successes and rumors like who did what to whom and who cheated on who.

The last type of party I work is with government officials and they're held at posh places, including Grand Central Terminal. They're usually stuffy, formal and boring. These people don't really talk; they just eat and smile. I guess politicians are careful about discussing private information in a public space because potential spies lurk everywhere.

Apparently, something happened years ago in an area of Grand Central known as the Whispering Gallery. It's a vaulted chamber right outside the Oyster Bar restaurant. The unique design of the Whispering Gallery's curved ceiling carries voices in such a way that they travel across the arch from one side of the room to another. You can stand in the corner diagonally across from someone and it sounds as if they're whispering over your shoulder. It's wild. So, understandably, politicos are careful of what they say at parties held in Grand Central.

During the Christmas season, servers slip from one party to another. I see countless Santas: fat ones, thin ones. Santas with bags full of presents, most of them fake, just for appearances. Even though these get-togethers take place in different locations, there's still a sort of sameness. They're all united in the fragrance of gingerbread and apple cider. I love seeing snowflakes lining the windows and streetlights glowing in the dark while I'm safe and snug inside. The holiday season affects those around us in a positive way. Cold, heartless New York City is more cheerful, infused with the Christmas spirit and a dash of empathy. But only temporarily.

The party I work another night is in the middle of Borough Park, Brooklyn, which is a sizable Hasidic Jewish enclave. *Strange place for a Christmas party,* I think. Maybe a Hanukkah party? Borough Park is home to one of the biggest Orthodox Jewish communities outside Israel and has one of the largest concentrations of Jews in the United States.

The address I'm given turns out to be a huge synagogue with a nice-sized basement space and an attached kitchen. The sprawling party room is separated in half by a long, tall, plastic rolling divider. On each side of the divider are six tables. There's another small table set for two at the head of each side of the room. Two

Chapter Six - Serving is Fun!

host tables? Weird. I soon discover that the small table is designed for a young married couple hold court. It appears I'm working an Orthodox Jewish wedding.

A young, good-looking server shakes my hand and introduces himself. Jacob is definitely not Orthodox (but probably Jewish) and friendly. As he gives me a tour, he explains the rules and the order of service. I'm already confused. In Orthodox Jewish weddings, the men and women are separated, he tells me. (Ah, that's the reason for two host tables on either side of the divider.) There's so much food with so many unfamiliar names. I only know a couple of them...kugel, kishka. The rest of the menu is difficult to remember, let alone pronounce.

Jacob senses my trepidation. With a smile says, "Don't worry, Maggie, you will get baptized tonight!" We both laugh. I'm glad Jacob and I have clicked. I think I've found my buddy for tonight. He helps a lot just by acknowledging that this isn't an easy event to work. I carry big trays on my shoulder weighed down with five heavy plates. They're extremely hot and I have no place to set down the tray. Jacob helps me hold the dishes and oversees the tray as I serve. We work as a seamless pair, which is much easier. The kitchen and the guests constantly rush us. They want fast service which isn't possible given the number of guests and the few number of servers. I only work one side of the room, the women's side. Each server is assigned one table. Just a handful of us have another person to help us. I'm lucky to have Jacob as my partner.

As a woman, I'm not allowed in the men's side of the room and that's fine with me. Except for Jacob, everyone ignores me and treats me poorly. I'm afraid I've made a mistake saying "yes" to this job. I promise myself not to come back again. The gig is getting crazier by the second because now there's dancing—men dancing with men beyond the partition and women dancing with women on my side of the wall. It's difficult to navigate the heavy trays around people dancing in a wild circle. We need to cross the room to get to the kitchen, amid the flailing arms and bodies. But nobody cares about the servers' dilemma.

The Kosher alcohol flows freely. Jacob hides a bottle behind a curtain and pours drinks for the two of us. We joke around, which eases the tension and helps the time pass quickly. When the alcohol hits me, instead of dark-suited, bearded Orthodox Jewish men, all I see is a roomful of Santa Clauses dancing beyond the partition. I share my thoughts with Jacob. "I want to scream 'Santa!'" I confess.

Jacob laughs and says, "You can say whatever you want. They won't understand you. They don't even know who Santa is." So much for my first Orthodox Jewish wedding and my cultural exchange crash course.

The next day, I wake up with a huge headache. The clock shows 1 p.m. It's afternoon already? I don't quite remember what happened last night besides serving at the Jewish wedding. The Kosher wine hit me like a brick. I check my phone and see a text from Jacob. "We did a good job and they want us for the next event," it says. I text him back, "As long as you keep pouring the wine... lol." With a smile on my face, I make coffee and get ready for another party. So much for my "never" doing another Orthodox Jewish wedding again. But Jacob—and the wine—helped make it bearable. A job is a job.

•

The last Christmas party of the year marks the end of the busy season. It's held at the Cathedral of St. John the Divine, a magnificent gothic-style Episcopal church in the Morningside Heights section of Manhattan. The largest church in the city, it's home to a wonderful gospel choir. This year, the company I work for is hired to serve a gathering of about 50 people.

I've never been inside the cathedral and I'm in awe of it. Like Saint Patrick's Cathedral in midtown but much, much larger. The architecture is more dramatic. My colleagues and I pass around food in one of St. John the Divine's impressive chambers which is decorated with a tall, stately Christmas tree. After *hors d'oeuvres*, we provide table service. The staff gets there early to set the elegant tables.

Guests begin arriving soon after. They gather in the cathedral for an incredibly moving gospel concert. We could hear them practicing as we set up the tables and even managed to steal away a few moments to watch them. I love the vibe in the cathedral. The atmosphere is friendly, welcoming and inclusive. Joyful, even. I finally feel the excitement of the season with Christmas and New Year's Day around the corner.

I take a breather and look back on the past year. I've worked hard and managed to support myself. This stirring, sacred place inspires me to thank God for looking out for me. Despite the challenges I faced, I feel fortunate to have come this far. I hope I'm blessed with an even better year ahead. I feel as though I'm getting closer and closer to achieving my American Dream. I just started working in the catering industry and managed to get into college so I can study the hospitality trade. I'm open to whatever the future brings. Most importantly, I'm able to do what I like. No more childcare and housekeeping for me! I vow to take small but successful steps, one by one, in my marathon run to successfully achieve my American Dream.

Chapter Seven
Office Failure

With the end of the busy holiday season fast approaching, I need to find something else to do in the new year. Although I studied international relations and the Middle Eastern culture in Poland, so far, it's been impossible to find work in my field. Again, I apply several times for positions at the United Nations but never get a response, let alone an interview. I guess they're not interested in a Polish girl with knowledge of the Arabic culture. Maybe they prefer someone from the region, which I understand completely. But no one even gives me a chance.

Growing up in Poland, besides studying the Middle East, I traveled to Israel, Egypt and other countries in the region. I became immersed in the history and politics of the area. I joined a group of young Poles gathered by the members of a Jewish Community Center connected to Nożyk Synagogue. Built in 1902, Nożyk Synagogue was the only surviving prewar Jewish house of prayer in Warsaw. At the community center, we studied Hebrew at ULPAN and promoted friendship between Christian Poles and Polish Jews.

I know I can use the knowledge and experience I gained at the Polish community center here in New York, but I'm wrong. Not a single soul is interested in me or my chosen profession in this city of experts. Maybe I should move to a more politically-oriented city…Washington, DC, for example. I can't be a babysitter or a server for the rest of my life. If those are the only areas I can find work, I'd prefer to go back to Europe and find a career that better suits me.

On the other hand, I love New York City. There's always something happening. It's fast-paced and exciting. This city has so much to offer. Just not to me. Not yet, anyway. I just need to find the right thing to do, the right career to utilize my skills set. I'm determined not to give up hope, yet I feel hopeless.

Maybe I'm just looking in the wrong place, I tell myself. On a whim, I click on the Polish Consulate's website. Who knows, they could have a job in my field. Seeing the white and red flag on the main page fills me with nostalgia for my homeland. *What would my career have looked like if I stayed in Poland?* I wonder. It would probably have been much easier since I could use my native tongue and local connections. Here, chasing the American Dream, I'm starting from scratch.

I remind myself of the reasons I decided to emigrate to the United States in the first place. For one, I crave challenges. Although during the last two years, I experienced moments of depression, I've also experienced incredible freedom. In those two years, though, I haven't felt fulfilled career-wise. Nothing gives me satisfaction. Maybe the challenge to become someone new is too big. Maybe I lost my self-esteem cleaning rich people's toilets.

The question, *"What the heck are you doing here, Maggie?"* echoes through my head. But behind that voice is another one telling me, *"Don't give up! Keep on trying!"* And here I am, back to Square One, still looking for the right opportunity, the right job. Again!

Chapter Seven - Office Failure

A posting on the Polish Consulate website catches my eye. *"A monthlong internship in the Consulate with the possibility of becoming an employee..."* it begins. This is perfect for me! With excitement and optimism, I click the "Apply" button.

located on Madison Avenue and East 37th Street, the Consulate of the Republic of Poland looks impressive. Built in 1902 in the Beaux-Arts style, it's one of the finest-looking buildings in Manhattan. I can easily imagine myself working there.

Walking through the heavy, carved wooden doors, I step into a magnificent hallway that immediately makes me feel important. There are tall columns, frescos and classical gilded décor throughout the entryway. The huge chandelier in the middle of the reception area reminds me of those found in the vintage buildings of Warsaw. I'm immediately transported back home; it's as though time doesn't exist. Again, I feel like Alice in Wonderland but instead of wanting to explore Tavern on the Green, I want to get lost in the Polish Consulate.

My eyes wander through the beautiful space, studying the crystal and gold. Out of nowhere, a deep man's voice pulls me back from my Polish daydream. "Hi! You must be Maggie," the sonorous voice says. "You have an appointment, right?"

"Yes, I'm here to be interviewed," I respond in Polish. It's good to see my communication skills in my native tongue are still sharp. Tomek, probably in his thirties, is handsome with delicately-carved features that sharply contrast with his booming voice. He beckons me to follow him.

Tomek takes me on a short tour of the building. As we walk through two grand-looking rooms, I have time to consider possible interview questions and my responses. I want to impress Tomek and his colleagues the same way this building has impressed me. I want to get the internship and hope it will lead to a permanent position, no matter what my responsibilities will be. Even scrubbing bathrooms. Because "if you can make it there, you'll make it anywhere."

Somehow, my determination and my blind optimism wins. I find the interview really easy. The questions are related to my cultural knowledge and political studies. I ace it.

It's Monday morning, the first day of my internship. I'm ready to start my dream job at the Polish Consulate's Department of Culture. I dress in my best work clothes, give myself a pep talk and head out the door. I'm tired, though, because I couldn't sleep the night before. A combination of nerves and excitement because this is important. This is a giant step in my career path. Getting the internship rebuilds my self-esteem, which is a great feeling. I want this feeling to stay with me forever. I picture myself as a young, career-hungry Polish New Yorker, quickly rising on the ladder toward her "American Dream."

The coffee I have at home doesn't help wake me up much. I consider buying another cup, but know I'll be short on money this month by taking on this unpaid internship. It's June and the party-catering season slows down for the summer. My serving job won't be enough to carry me through, so I need to be extra careful with cash. Truthfully, I'm scared about my financial situation.

Fuck it! I tell myself. *This is my first day of an important position at an important institution. I need to celebrate.* I decide to order the biggest cup of coffee Starbucks offers to say cheers to my bright future in international relations. The coffee line is long and it's taking more time than I expected. I feel stress in the air; everyone is in a rush. Even me. The faces are tense as they scowl at their phones. There's no interaction with anyone else, as if they don't notice anyone. People are hyper-focused on themselves.

Chapter Seven - Office Failure

The cold reality of a Manhattan morning hits me. I'm not sure if I want to be a part of this rat race. But on the other hand, there's a sense of power behind single-mindedness. There's a sort of strength in their firm professionalism. It makes me feel part of something, something greater and more significant than myself. Shit, I feel important today too! I *am* important! I put on my Manhattan poker face and decide to conquer the world as I step into my first day as an intern at the Polish Consulate.

My little desk is full of stuff. Papers are scattered everywhere. To familiarize myself with the position, I pick up one and read about the last cultural event held at the Consulate, a piano concert. Suddenly, a voice behind me says, "We have so many emails that need to be checked. Just delete the ones you think aren't important."

How the hell am I supposed to know what's important and what's not important? I ask myself. *It's my first day here!* Cheerfully, I respond, "Sure, I will." My computer is so old, it should be given a decent burial. It takes forever to boot up and is snail slow at processing. But I keep working, determined to complete my initial task quickly and efficiently. Time crawls by. I can't wait for my break. I'm buried under tons of emails, most of which can be discarded without even opening. After reading through a few, I decide to trash them all. Success!

I've finished my first task, yet there's no applause. I only feel warmth breath on my neck. Anna, the coordinator, is standing close enough to check my work. A tall, skinny, blonde in her early forties, Anna stands so close I can smell her too-sweet, flowery perfume.

"That was fast," she comments with a hint of sarcasm. "Hopefully you didn't delete anything important." Then she gives me a snarky smile, knowing exactly that I have. I bet I wasn't the first one to have done this.

Pointing at a tall metal filing cabinet, Anna adds, "We also need to organize this." I'm horrified at the sheer size—and boredom—of my next task. "I'm pretty sure there's important paperwork in there. Some of the files probably go back to before the civil wars," she remarks. *Shit, that was the 1980s,* I remember. *Those files must be a mess!*

Sensing my horror, Anna tells me, "But why don't you take a break? Go get something to eat with the other interns." I do as Anna suggests.

I soon learn that four interns have been taken on for the month. Besides me, there are two women and one guy. They're spending the summer in Manhattan for this internship before going back home to Poland. The three of them are still students, making me the oldest. My first impression is that they're rude, loud and immature. They have the attitude that nothing is impossible to accomplish. They're extremely optimistic with no filters—they say whatever they think. And it's clear that they think this monthlong internship will change their entire lives. With a New York City internship under their belts, job opportunities in Poland will abound.

My world, on the other hand, isn't viewed through rose-colored glasses. I've been in America on and off for several years. I've cleaned dog poop. I've changed dirty sheets. I've served *pate* to drunken stockbrokers. I look at life more realistically and less optimistically, from the perspective of someone who lives the New York City reality. Life here is fast, furious and expensive. And that's on a good day!

I count the money in my pocket. That's all the spending money I have for the week. Maybe the young students' energy will feed me the rest of the week. Maybe their enthusiasm will rub off on me. I like their positive vibes and giddy talk; it relaxes me. They find everything thrilling. They aren't jaded by life yet and that's refreshing.

The simple sushi lunch we share and just walking the Manhattan streets is a huge source of pleasure to them.

Chapter Seven - Office Failure

To see the city through other people's eyes, people new to it, is a joy for me too. I enjoy talking about "my city" to them. Yes, New York City is "my city" now. I know quite a bit about its history and culture. I feel like a private tour guide. In fact, I'm not sure which "job" I enjoy more: intern or tour guide. The second one is directly related to what I'm currently studying in college: tourism and hospitality. I think I've made a fine choice.

Back at the Polish Consulate, I tackle the heavy file cabinet crammed with old papers dating as far back as 20 years. Most cover cultural issues or are reports from international events. Besides the documents, the metal drawers are full of dust that probably dates back 100 years before the papers. There might even be a copy of the US Constitution hidden there. Accompanying the disintegrating papers and dust is an attractive stench that brings to mind a pile of old, rotten rags.

My eyes start to itch. *This is not how I imagined my internship,* I tell myself. All I do is clean. Either I'm cleaning out emails from an inbox or cleaning out a junky file cabinet. It looks like housekeeping has found me yet again, this time at the Polish Consulate. Disheartened and upset, I'm about to cry.

Once more, I my heart travels to Poland. I try to imagine what I would be doing in Warsaw if only I had stayed. Sifting through the mess of files, I think of my family. Out of nowhere, my uncle's name pops up on one of the papers. Am I hallucinating? I wipe my eyes to see more clearly but it's not an illusion. His name is still there. I hold in my hand my uncle's speech from a decade ago about the Polish-Jewish cultural relationship. I know he used to travel to the United States as a journalist, but I had no idea he'd addressed the Polish Embassy in Washington, DC. He was an expert on Polish-Jewish issues and rebuilding the relationship between these two groups in Poland. He also studied Poland's diaspora after the communist period. Although my uncle's speech is ten years old, it seems as though it were written at that very moment—and dedicated to me. I take it as a sign that I should stay in the States. That I'm exactly where I belong.

Suddenly everything that felt strange becomes more familiar. It's as though I'm looking at the world through a microscope instead of a telescope and the distance between my homeland and New York City has vanished. My homesickness is gone, and I have hope again. Somehow, my uncle sends me a message from ten years in the past. From him, I learn that even in the dust we can find something new and fresh to love and believe in.

That's when I decide not to give up on my boring internship and carry it through until the end. I hope I'll gain more skills than cleaning out file cabinets. Maybe patience and the idea that everything is a learning experience will be my lessons.

•

Weeks pass. I do whatever I'm asked at the Polish Consulate. Some of it interesting, some of it boring as hell. But whatever my task, I'm determined to do it cheerfully. And well. Often, I'm asked to review paperwork and add my opinion. I translate documents from English to Polish and do Department of Culture-related work. I'd love to be involved organizing cultural events but besides a piano concert, little is scheduled during the summer. It's not the most exciting job I've ever had but it's also not the worst.

After the internship is over, I am offered a position at the Consulate that's opening soon. I'm flattered they appreciate my work—though I'm not thrilled with the work. "Thank you," I tell them diplomatically, with a smile. "I'll consider it."

The truth is that during the past month, I realize I'm not an office person. I burn out easily. I get bored quickly. I need to stay more physically active. My moment of truth comes when I have to type on a typewriter. Yes, a typewriter! Even though it's an electric typewriter, I'm still in shock that I have to use such an antiquated machine. At the Consulate, they still use typewriters to add to or make corrections to documents. I just can't believe it. There's got to be a better way. After all, this is the 21st century. Even at the Polish Consulate.

Everything seems so old there, from before the dinosaurs walked the earth. The atmosphere is smothering and archaic. The old-fashioned rules are set in stone with no room for improvement—or growth. It reminds me why I left Poland in the first place—a free spirit, I find it hard to conform to such rigidity.

At the heart of all I do, propelling me forward, is the quest for my American Dream. Isn't New York City the place where dreams become reality? That's what the songs and movies tell you. But I know that my American Dream can't be found working at the Polish Consulate.

"Thank you," I politely tell Anna, the internship coordinator. I proudly accept my internship certificate and give her a handshake. But I turn down her job offer at the Polish Consulate. With a twinge of regret, I leave my culture and my career in diplomacy behind.

•

I know exactly what I will do next: be a tour guide. I need a job that's active, not passive, and keeps me on the move. Working in an office makes me feel useless. It's a waste of my energy and my skills set. I enjoy interacting with people. I excel at it, actually. I need to be outdoors, not cooped up in a stuffy office.

Many people associate success in New York City with corporate life. But to me, cubicle life is suffocating. Performing the same routines each day is comforting for some, but it makes me feel trapped. I came to the United States to learn who I was, to explore and grow. I can't find growth sorting through papers (even if my uncle wrote them!), collating documents and refilling staplers. I came here seeking personal growth in the wilds of the New York City streets.

When it comes right down to it, I'm a people person. I really enjoyed giving that lunchtime tour to my fellow interns around Manhattan. I love this city's colorful history and architecture. New York City has so much European influence in culture and style, yet it has its own distinct personality. I love sharing the magical energy of the city that never sleeps with people who always dreamed of visiting it. I want to "sell" the city and my own personal story, to become part of the Big Apple's fabric.

This city is built on dreams. Every single one of us contributes to it. We are all part of that dream and the New York City story. I can't wait to tell mine as a tour guide.

Chapter Eight
A Tour Guide Career

It's late August and I'm searching the Polish newspapers for work, any type of work. I know what I want to do but I'm not sure if I'm ready to be a tour guide. Why? For one thing, my English sucks. To become a card-carrying New York City Tour Guide, I must pass a test. Even to work on one of those "hop on, hop off" buses. And the written test is pretty hard. They ask all sorts of obscure questions like Jackie O's address.

I research the possibility of becoming a tour guide. As much as I want to dive headlong into that career, it's impossible right now. Again, I'm disappointed: in the world, in myself. Broke and depressed, I look for anything to make money. My frustration reaches its peak. With a loud "Fuck it!," I toss away the newspaper. Tears stream down my cheeks. I'm tired of spiraling, constantly pursuing useless opportunities.

I'm such a loser that don't even have a tissue to wipe my face. I grab the closest thing: the newspaper I just crumbled up and threw to the floor. *Whatever,* I grumble, and bring the clump of paper up to my face. What? I can't believe it! There's an ad on the page that reads: "Polish travel agency Polonez seeks the right candidate for a tour guide position...." Am I dreaming? Nope, the ad is real alright. That's it! I know this job is already mine. Once again, just as I'm about to give up, something saves me.

I immediately apply for the position and get an interview the next day. I do my best to look sharp, wearing jeans and a not-too-formal blouse with a not-too-formal blue jacket. I want to look casual but confident. The interview is in Greenpoint, a Polish community in Brooklyn. I haven't been in Greenpoint for a long time and I'm excited to see Poles again. And eat Polish food! Greenpoint is full of wonderful Polish delis, grocery stores, even liquor stores. There's also lots of old Slavic ladies with *babushka* scarves on their heads.

The G train takes at least an hour. I know I'm approaching Greenpoint when I hear people speaking Polish on the train. The car is full of Slavic chatter, while others sleep deeply, trying to get rest between shifts. The men's clothes are covered with paint splatters and sheetrock dust, day laborers, I guess, construction workers on their way home after a long day's work. The train is crowded. We stand so close to each other that I can smell alcohol on the breath of some of the workers. I'm glad the ride is almost over; any longer and I might get drunk just from breathing the same air.

The dusty construction workers pile off the train at Greenpoint Avenue, just like I do. We flood the station in a single stream and I'm stuck between them, feeling lost. What a huge difference from midtown, where everyone is so well put together. The sound of the streets reminds me of Warsaw. The people are a mix of old, traditionally-dressed Polish folks and young hipsters who have recently moved to this remote area because it's cheap. It's a place where the conventional meets the future. I like it.

Greenpoint moves in super slo-mo. The pace is lazier. On street corners, young Gen-Xers lean against bricks buildings, smoking pot. Don't they even have jobs? Or is this their job? The tang of marijuana mixes with the aroma of Polish soul food. The lazy late-summer afternoon and the muted sunlight makes the street scene look impressionistic—a multifaceted painting of sights, sounds and scents. I'm trying to capture the moment, remember it, and for a second, I've traveled to another dimension. I quickly snap out of it, reminding myself that I'm not here to visit but for an interview. Sandwiched in between the kielbasa (sausage) store and a pierogi (dumplings) shop, I find Polonez Travel Agency.

I know I'll be a good fit. I already have tour guiding experience in Poland. During summers in high school, I was a guide in one of its old castles. I loved taking people through the Niedzica's ancient chambers and narrow, winding staircases. I was happy to share my knowledge about Niedzica and its role in Polish history. I even made up a few stories and spiced up others to make them more interesting. Sometimes I'd even get one of my friends to hide in a dark corner, pretending to be a ghost. People loved it! And I loved the attention I was getting. Plus, I'm not shy about talking in front of a crowd. Just the opposite, I thrive on it.

And now, on the other side of the Atlantic, I look forward to showing tourists all the cool things about New York City. Whenever I have free time, I go off exploring. I'd jump at the chance to show people around Manhattan—and get paid for it. It would be great to share my favorite places and stories about New York with Polish visitors—for pay.

As soon as I open Polonez's door, a musty odor hits me. It's the aroma of old fabric and new dust. The place is messy, practically falling apart. I bet it's never been cleaned, let alone renovated. Polonez reminds me of a storage facility crossed with a knick-knack shop. Dolls wearing red and white dresses decorated with Polish flags are everywhere. Souvenirs from a bunch of States are scattered all over this place. There are posters from

Niagara Falls, the Statue of Liberty and the Lincoln Memorial covering the peeling wallpaper. But even they don't hide the ugliness of this place.

For a moment, I doubt Polonez and I will be a match. Like the neighborhood itself, the agency looks as if it's torn from a different century. There are many areas like this in New York, specific in their ethnicity. You can travel through the city's five boroughs and travel around the world: Chinatown, Little Italy, Koreatown. But that's the beauty of the New York smorgasbord. I want my tours to focus on this unique New York City cultural mishmash. There's adventure everywhere. You just have to know where to look. And I do.

Seated at the desk facing the door is a comical-looking guy. He's short, bald and round. His head sinks deep into his shoulders as though it's too heavy for his body. As he cleans his filthy glasses on a shirttail, he treats me to a very judgmental look. "You must be the potential contestant," he says with a sly smile, as if I'm a participant in his own private beauty pageant.

"Contestant for what?" I shoot back, annoyed. The feminist in me responds with an aggressive reaction to his stupid joke. I'm very familiar with the Polish macho man's way of making inappropriate comments. He thinks he's funny. This is his way of flirting and he's convinced it's acceptable to do so. Should I just ignore his sexist comment? Or leave? Or maybe sue him? I play dumb and flash my brightest smile, telling him, "I'm the best one. Look at me, I've already won the contest."

Behind his freshly-polished glasses, his bloodshot blue eyes look surprised. I decide to play his game. I'll stay and go toe-to-toe with him. I almost forgot how powerful that weapon called "flirt" is. I'm not proud of myself for stooping to his level, but he's going to pay for his sexist sarcasm. I can tell he's shocked at my response because he's more serious now. He starts my job interview in earnest.

He shoots questions about my personal tour guide experience and about customer service in general. It covers handling difficult situations and finding the right solutions more than anything else. I must give him the right answers because his smile gets bigger and bigger. "Okay," he says. "The job is yours."

"Excellent," I tell him. "Maybe I can start with some of my favorite places in Manhattan like…"

He holds up one hand. "Whoa, whoa." I stop talking. "This weekend you're going to Niagara Falls as an assistant guide, to learn. The next tour will be on your own." He pauses then adds, "I hope you can handle 47 people. That's how big tomorrow's tour is."

"No problem," I tell him. His last words resonate in my head and scare the crap out of me. *Forty-seven freaking people?!* I worry. "In my last job, I'd look after 100 people," I lie. Where the heck did that come from? Oh, right, Aunt Basia: "If you fake it, you will make it!" Her credo has taken me this far. It will take me even further. For example, nine hours north of Greenpoint, to Niagara Falls.

Fast forward one week. I sit in the front seat of tour bus with my driver on the left and almost 50 strangers behind me. With a little help from my driver (if necessary), I lead the first tour on my own. Last weekend's trip to Niagara Falls went well. I learned a lot from Caroline, the guide leading the group. Now I'm on my own.

I can't stop thinking of Caroline, though. She was vivacious, attractive and always smiling. She approached every single person in the group with patience and warmth. A typical, Polish-looking girl—tall, with pale skin, blonde hair and blue eyes—Caroline also had American confidence. Her self-assurance indicated that she'd been in the States for some time already.

Caroline was very friendly. She clearly knew how to entertain people. She made jokes and encouraged people to participate in ridiculous games during the long drive. She had a good rap about the places we passed on the way road as we traveled through New York, New Jersey, and Pennsylvania. There were interesting stories connected to many US states and about Niagara Falls itself. Also in Caroline's repertoire were facts and legends related to Native Americans and pioneer settlements.

Among her other duties was "babysitting." She made sure no one got lost and because of their poor English communication skills, helped them buy souvenirs and personal items. Most of our clientele is visiting from Poland and they need to be on an organized tour because of the language barrier.

I had no idea adult childcare would be one of my responsibilities. I thought my babysitting days were behind me! So, I'm basically a translator and server instead of an actual tour guide, which turns out to be a very tiny aspect of the job. Helping customers get what they need, looking after them…it sounds like I'm a kindergarten teacher. And honestly, it's much easier to babysit kids than adults. Kids tend to listen to you, while adults don't listen at all. Instead, they constantly argue with what you say. It's exhausting. The dark side of my new job is revealed during my training weekend training. I hope I'm cut out for it.

Caroline's shining example rings in my tired brain a week later as I lead my first solo tour. I'm a shepherd gathering a flock of Polish sheep from a Greenpoint, Brooklyn street. It takes forever to board the bus. Why? Because everyone suddenly decides they have to either go to the bathroom or have a cigarette before the long drive. I go over the rules, terms and conditions of the tour. But first, I introduce myself and talk about Polonez, which is the oldest agency serving Polish travelers in New York.

Already, we're behind schedule. I hope to catch up on the road. My driver, Mike, a attractive, young man, promises me we'll get to Niagara Falls on time. "Not a big deal. I drive fast," he assures me. I don't know if I should be glad or afraid.

I loosen up once we hit the New York State Thruway. Mike is a fast but careful driver. Stressed at the beginning of the trip, I feel confident now knowing we'll make it on time. All the passengers seem friendly. For the most part, they follow my rules—except during our frequent breaks. They're never back on the bus when they're supposed to be. A 10-minute break extends to 15 minutes or more. The worst are cigarette breaks; they take the longest. (Why do all Poles seem to smoke?) My explanation that we're on a tight schedule, so we must be on time doesn't work with this group. Their response is: "We want to enjoy what we paid for." Man, it's going to be a long two days!

They sneak alcohol on the bus, which is *really* breaking the rules. I'm afraid they'll be shitfaced before we even get to Niagara Falls. Their response? "We want to relax. It's what we paid for."

My response? "I'm trying do my job. It's what *I* get paid for." We reach an understanding and move forward. The more time we spend taking breaks the less time we'll have at the Falls. They finally understand this concept. I'm glad we have no other issues on the road and that my driver is always able to catch up.

After nine hours the bus finally arrives at Niagara Falls State Park. It's late afternoon and to my surprise, nobody wants to leave the bus. You'd think they'd want to stretch, but no. They're comfy, cozy—and drunk. Even after my lecture, they snuck sips of vodka in the back of the bus, ignoring Polonez's strict "no-alcohol on board" rule.

They act like I'm spoiling their fun, pushing them out of the bus to enjoy what many consider the honorary eighth wonder of the world. The fresh, cool air and the sound of 3,000 tons of water crashing against the rocks sober them up right away. Now, they jockey for position, pushing to the front of the line for a better view of the Falls. But there's no "bad" view. From all angles, it's spectacular, a 3-D postcard. For the moment, everyone is satisfied.

More than 75,000 gallons of water per second flows over Niagara Falls at Horseshoe Falls, which is the largest of the three that comprise Niagara Falls. (The American Falls and Bridal Veil Falls being the other two.) This makes it the biggest waterfall in the United States and one of the largest in the world.

We stand in a long queue at one of the viewpoints, in silence, in awe. But the quiet only lasts seconds. Then I hear just one word, in English, coming from the crowd: "Wow!" The adventure is back!

"So, the long bus ride paid off, right?" I say loudly, flashing them a sarcastic smile.

Next stop, Maid of the Mist, the boat that will take us as close to the Falls possible. I try to do a headcount, but my charges are bouncing around like excited pinballs. "Stop moving, I'm trying to count!" I shout. I have to make sure no one's missing before we board the boat.

After the numbers line up, we each get a disposable blue raincoat to keep us dry. I laugh to myself; my group looks like an army of Polish Smurfs. They melt in with the other visitors, who are dressed exactly the same way. Damn! It will be hard to keep track of them since they all look alike. A hundred blue creatures swarm the grounds. One calls, "Hey Maggie, where's your Papa Smurf?" We all laugh. Hey, this might not be so bad after all.

The boat ride is fast. It only takes 15 minutes for the Maid of the Mist to reach the Falls. As we get closer, the sound of the cascade gets louder. It's deafening and you can't hear a thing besides roaring water. You can't even hear the person beside you, the Falls are so thunderous. You can't even hear your own thoughts! But there is this odd moment of nothingness between the water's crashing sound. If you listen closely, there's a second of stillness in the air.

For a moment I freeze and the noise unites with the silence. Besides the Falls, all I can hear is my own breath. I realize how fast I'm breathing. Am I panicking? No, I feel calm. It must be the adrenaline from seeing such a breathtaking sight. No words are spoken; no words are necessary. I look around. All I see is a big, collective, silent wow! I can't hear voices anymore, though people's mouths are moving. I just see the silent "wow" on their faces. It's pretty incredible.

Water is everywhere: inside the boat, on all surfaces, on our shiny, blue raincoats. We are so close to the Falls. Dangerously close, it seems. Like I can almost touch them. How would that feel? Then I pull out of my thoughts as the boat chugs away from the Falls.

Suddenly, the sound is back. The excited chatter of those who got soaked surrounds me. Everyone starts moving about the boat either trying to stay dry or running toward the mist to get bathed in it. Life is back. Birds fly around us, a reminder that nature thrives here. We humans are so small, so insignificant in this vast, wild world.

I look at my group. They are all wet but content. The cheap raincoats don't help much. But then again, I think they all wanted to get wet. I'm happy just to see them happy. With a hint of irony in my voice, I ask, "Is this what you paid for?" They respond with laughter.

We still have a few more sights to see in Niagara Falls today. One is taking a closer view from the American side of the Falls from a staircase. It's a well-known spot where the movie *Niagara* was filmed in 1953, starring Marilyn Monroe. The other "must" is seeing Niagara Falls illuminated after dark. Another breathtaking sight. There's an extraordinary multicolored light show that reflects off the cascades and mist, making it even more mysterious and ethereal. I take my charges to see both sights. Of course, they love them. Who wouldn't? Even half-drunken Poles. This should be enough adventure for the time being.

At the end of our first day in Niagara Falls, it's finally time to relax. Tomorrow will be chock full of other activities. Exhausted but happy, my tour group arrives at the hotel. It's late and we're all dreaming of a nice, long sleep. But it doesn't look as though sleep will come anytime soon. We're in a long line with three tour groups ahead of us.

After almost 30 minutes of waiting, I finally hold the room keys in my hand. I keep counting and recounting them. There's one missing: mine. It appears that I don't have lodgings for tonight. (Did Polonez do this on purpose to save money on my room?) It's frustrating but at this point, I'm so tired that I don't care. I'll sleep in the lobby or on the bus.

But Mike, my driver, comes to the rescue. He offers to share his double room with me. Exhausted, I go straight to bed without even undressing. I know that in five hours, I'll have to get up again, so I don't want to waste any precious time. Since nobody knows my room number, no one will bother me. Hopefully, I can squeeze in a few hours of deep, restful sleep.

I'm up early to make sure everything is in order. I want to have enough time to prepare myself for another challenging day of playing tour guide to a bunch of unruly Poles. Mike is already gone when I wake up, probably getting our chariot ready for the road. I go down to the lobby to grab a coffee, hoping for a few more stolen moments. But it looks like everyone else is up too. They've already had breakfast and are packed, ready to roll. Well, no "me time" this morning. I dash back upstairs to get my bag.

One last headcount before boarding the bus. Oops! The number of people standing before me doesn't match the number on my list. I'm missing five. One of my charges tells me Room 666 had a party last night. "God, they were so loud!" someone else adds.

I storm off to check the room. Thankfully, the front desk had the foresight to give me extra keys so I can let myself in. But first, I try calling the room several times. No answer. I bang on the door. No answer. The minute I unlock the door, I'm surrounded by the sickening stench of alcohol. All five of the missing Poles are crashed out all over the place. They sleep on the floor, in the bathtub, on the bed, giving no sign of life. Shit, I hope they're not dead! That would suck.

I gently pull on the arm closest to me. No response. I shake him more vigorously. That wakes him up, but just for a moment. He turns onto his other side and goes back to sleep. I try yelling. Nothing. I try pleading. Still nothing. By this point, I'm stewing. "Fine! We're going in 15 minutes," I yell. "If you're not on the bus by then, I'm leaving without you. Then you'll have to find your way back to Brooklyn on your own." Still nothing. "I mean it!"

Shocked and still drunk, this finally gets a reaction. Their already pale Slavic complexions get even more white. They're even whiter than the walls. United in panic, they jump up like soldiers under command. I've never seen people pack up so quickly. They probably forget half their belongings. But at this point, I don't care. It's on them.

In a drunken rush, they trip on the empty vodka bottles that litter the floor and make their way to the door. As pathetic as the situation is, I can't stop laughing. They look so wacky. But I was dead serious about leaving them behind. I meant it. We don't have the time for nonsense and the schedule is already tight as it is. We have a long drive back home and there are still two attractions to visit.

I recount my group and the numbers line up this time. "All set! We can leave," I pipe with false optimism in my voice.

When I ask Mike how he's doing this morning, he gives me a stoic, "Fine."

"It looks like we're a little behind schedule," I say, making sure he knows.

"Not a big deal! I'll drive fast." Mike comforts me yet again. This time, I know that indeed, he's a reliable driver, speedy yet safe.

The trip back home takes longer than I expect. Along the way, we stop to see two more sights—Fort Niagara and the Corning Museum of Glass. Our pace is harried now because the group is anxious to get home. The most exciting part of the trip is over.

Mike is great. He knows how to avoid traffic by taking side roads when necessary. During these past two days, we had a chance to get to know each other and became friends. He's very macho on the outside but a real softie on the inside. A simple guy who doesn't talk much but listens and observes. Mike is very ambitious, professional and helpful. He's wonderful to work with and steps up when needed. When people dilly-dallying at one of the stops, in a firm voice Mike tells them, "I'm leaving in five minutes. Whoever wants to come with me, jump on right now!" And then he gives me a wink.

Mike admits this kind of thing is common—someone always takes advantage. Plus. there's always someone who isn't satisfied. They expect a lot but don't generally give tips for good service. Mike also says that I need to be much firmer with them. Straight and to the point. I should *inform* and not *ask*. "Never give them Option A or B to choose from because it's going to create chaos instead of giving solutions," he suggests. "Always give them only one option and if we have time for another attraction, then then tell them, 'We have a surprise!'" I really value his advice, especially when he adds. "You have to be a leader." He finishes and focuses on the road. I sigh and sink deeper into the seat and try to relax.

I look forward to getting back home. I'm exhausted from the road and from corralling almost 50 adults who often behave like kids. It's overwhelming, especially for my first solo tour guide venture. I look back and analyze the whole trip. Overall, I feel positive about it. In general, everything went smoothly. We were pretty much on time. There were no accidents. (Not yet!)

But my quiet reflections are interrupted by the sound of grinding metal followed by a growl coming from the engine. The bus stops and Mike yells, "Fuck!" For the first time in this often-stressful trip, my calm, stoic driver curses. I'm not a mechanic. All I can do is give him a smile, hoping it will help. Mike smiles back. "Don't worry it will be fast." He goes outside to figure out what's wrong.

Forty-seven people descend upon me with questions. What happened? When will we get back? Since I'm in charge, they expect me to know the answers, but I don't. Instead, I point out how close we are to home. We can see Manhattan. "Home, it's there," I tell them, trying to diffuse the situation. "It's right there in front of us. Look how beautiful it shines in the dark." The illuminated skyscrapers loom in front of us. We aren't even an hour away.

Fascinated by the view, they stop asking. But just for a second. From the back of the bus, someone shoots a bullet toward me: "Yeah, it looks awesome but when are we going to get there? Should we walk?" I don't know what to tell them.

Relief comes as Mike boards the bus. After strange noises and more cursing from him outside, he's finally back. We look at him with hope and expectation. "It's not a quick fix," he sighs, exasperated. Besides being an excellent driver, Mike is also mechanic. "There's a broken part that needs to be replaced," he explains. Mike calls Polonez to tell them what happened. They're sending another driver with the necessary part. It's going to take another three to four hours before we get moving. The passengers are annoyed. The stunning New York City skyline is so close yet so far. By some miracle, we make it home before dawn, more or less in one piece.

•

The fall travel season draws an end and winter is coming quickly. The East Coast is soon covered with an (early) blanket of snow, and then it starts snowing again. November days are dark and short. Before Thanksgiving, New York is less crowded with tourists and for some reason, more romantic. The November sunsets are always spectacular. It's the angle of the sun, I'm told. People seem to walk faster as winter approaches, seeking a respite with hot chocolate or coffee in hand. Bars and restaurants are filled with people looking for companionship and shelter from the storm. Most of them are locals.

The city takes a breather from the next wave of tourists. Manhattan, all decked out for Christmas, will soon be invaded. The streets surrounding Rockefeller Center, with its famous ice-skating rink and towering Christmas tree, will become almost impassable. The gaudy, decorated windows of Saks Fifth Avenue will draw crowds. It's as predictable as the tides.

With the change of seasons, I have a brief break before the catering season revs up again. For me, fall is sort of wistful. I'm done with my tour-guiding for the year; it's pretty much a spring and summertime thing. Since my fateful solo trip to Niagara Falls, I learned a great deal. I can finally unwind and have weekends to myself. In the last three months, every single Saturday and Sunday was spent taking people on tours around Manhattan or on bus trips to Washington, DC, Philadelphia, Boston and Pennsylvania Dutch Country. It was fun but exhausting.

I'm not sure how many faces I saw, steps I took or camera-clicks I heard. But I miss it. Some trips were better than others. Some groups behaved better than others. For the most part, I got decent tips from both the customers and Polonez. They already told me that they want me back next year. After a rocky start, I learned how to control people and difficult situations. I've been told that I interact well with the customers, provide them with interesting chatter and have an engaging personality. My boss complimented my storytelling prowess, which is one reason I decide to continue my college studies in tourism and hospitality. I might finally be riding the train that will take me to the right destination this time.

And that station that is called, "The American Dream and Success."

Chapter Nine
More Opportunities—and Failures

Both of my professions—tour guiding and catering—benefit me in my quest for a career in the hospitality trade. Why? Because they're all about customer service, feeling confident speaking to large groups and serving the public. I learn how to approach clients, satisfy their needs and solve issues. I like what I do, and it seems that people like me too. Other travel agencies besides Polonez have taken me on.

Over the next few years, I work for a number of tourism companies. I take groups not only around the Northeast but all the way down to Florida twice a year. It requires strong leadership and organizational skills and most importantly, patience. Spending two weeks in Florida moving from place to place with a group of 20 or 30 can be a blast—or it can be a nightmare. It depends on the people in your group as well as the itinerary.

Some tours go nicely and others, not so much. There are always some who criticize everything. I kindly refer to them as "The Complainers"—and not so kindly call them "The Assholes." They expect more than I—or anyone other human being—can give them. Sometimes it gets so crazy I need my driver to intervene. But most of the time, I make friends with the people in my group. In fact, I still stay in touch with some of them.

With private tours made up of families, couples or individuals, it's easier to connect. You get to know your clients and are able to give them your undivided attention. I prefer these types of tours, although they take more time and energy to prepare. But they're more specific, more focused. For example, some zero in on architecture while others concentrate on modern art or street art, especially murals. The client expects more than just a generalized history, which they can get by visiting these places on their own. Since they pay more for these personalized tours, I give them more. For instance, more of my time and knowledge, as well as bonuses like insider stories. Because my full focus is on them, we always have time for "extras," seeing additional attractions and taking longer lunches, coffee or beer breaks.

Most of the time I'm invited to accompany them for a meal or snack. During these breaks, they pump me for more info about the big city, not only about visiting places but they ask about my personal life. They want to see New York from the perspective of someone who lives here. This is the best way to learn. I happily share my perspective. It makes me feel like I'm an US ambassador to the Polish traveler.

In addition to tour-guiding, I work for more than one catering company. I wear many hats: server, service captain, bartender and kitchen prep worker. We operate both large events and intimate, private parties held in customers' homes. Each time I work a catering gig, I learn a new skill. Every company has their own set of standards and it's a challenge trying to accommodate them. But this teaches me how to be flexible and think on my feet.

My college education adds to my confidence. I know how to "surf" from one corner of the tourism and hospitality industry into the other. My instructors tell me I'm one of the best students in the CUNY program because I've learned the tourism business from all sides, including the catering and food industry, which is my major.

I graduated two years earlier with honors and I'm working in the field, gaining more experience daily. Now I'm qualified to train restaurant workers and run a catering operation. This is what I want to do next—run my own catering business. And I will! I thrive on the craziness of the kitchen and see myself working there one day too.

•

In the past couple of years, I tried to accomplish something else on my own—but without success. My failure is probably because I wasn't ready for the opportunity presented to me. The time wasn't right. You see, I had the chance to buy a travel agency for a very reasonable price. The offer comes when my boss Elisa decides to move and sell her business. I'm flattered that she sees me as a potential buyer.

At the time, I was doing a few hours of internship a week at Eliza's travel agency. Basically, I try my hand as a travel agent, selling airline tickets to her loyal customers. Her client base consists of a small group of Polish people, old-school Poles who aren't comfortable purchasing airline tickets online themselves. Most of them are senior citizens who need everything done for them. They have to talk to a physical travel agent to book their flights, hotels, car rentals, the whole deal.

This type of job requires good listening skills and 24/7 availability. These oldsters always want to chit-chat and never seem to sleep. Although the work isn't bad, I can't give that kind of time commitment while studying and working catering gigs. Answering phones and doing constant research on the best travel deals for a handful of customers is not what I'm looking for. I can't imagine running a travel agency, doing this day after day. I'd pull out my hair!

I admit, I'm not the best office worker and owning a travel agency requires you to spend looooong hours in the office. The idea of *owning* a travel agency is fantastic, like an American Dream, but the thought of actually *running* one is not. I know I won't be able to do it. Besides, there's no money in it. And no future. This is the 21st century; everyone has internet access. So, traditional travel agencies will soon die. So, my fantasy of owning a prosperous travel agency dies too.

The previous winter, I tried working in Polonez's office. Boy, was that a mistake! I forgot how bad I was at sitting behind a desk all day. I tried to keep things orderly but I just couldn't. Paperwork is not my friend! I make mistakes when filling out documents and always miss something. It's incredibly frustrating and the end of the workday can't come soon enough. I give it my best shot but after two months I ultimately give up and quit.

•

Another time, I try to open my own catering business. What a total failure! I'm just not ready to run a catering company. I don't have the required organizational skills or the necessary certificates. Or the money and time to invest in a venture like this. All I have is an aspiration.

My business partner, Anna, shares the same dream with me. We know each other from catering and are confident we can do it, no problem. Although we share a strong drive to achieve, to open our own business, we aren't well prepared. We are trained in serving, not running a business. We also don't make an informed decision about the community we wish to serve—the Polish population in Greenpoint, Brooklyn.

Chapter Nine - More Opportunities—and Failures

Don't get me wrong, Poles are partiers, but they don't necessarily have a lot of money. Besides, they're so steeped in tradition, Anna and I soon discover that they prefer making the dishes themselves from old family recipes. For large gatherings, they tend to do potlucks or rent space in a restaurant that already provides food and service. What a rude awakening for us!

It's a sad revelation that catering isn't popular among the Poles in Greenpoint. Not yet, anyway. After trying to negotiate prices with a handful of Polish clients, Anna and I decide to close the business. Our potential customers have lofty expectations but not the money to back it up. We don't have the time or energy to chase our pipe dream, so we give it up.

So, as you can see, I've tried careers in both tourism and hospitality, but it doesn't work out. I'm not ready, I tell myself. But is readiness part of achieving your American Dream? Isn't it about trying repeatedly, failing and learning in the process?

Every time I try to accomplish something, I go too far. My dreams are too cumbersome, too unreasonable, too far from reality. I'm starting to lose faith.

Chapter Ten
A College Career

"Serve from the left, clean from the right!" This is what I keep reminding my students. Yes, *my* students. That's right, I'm teaching.

But no matter how much I repeat this mantra, my pupils confuse serving sides. I'm getting tired of reminding them repeatedly. Months into the semester, this class, these students, are not my best. Although they have a love for cooking, their serving skills stink. They prefer to be in the kitchen hanging out with the back of the house students instead of with their classmates at the front of the house. (FYI, "back of the house" is trade talk for the kitchen and "front of the house" refers to the serving area or restaurant.) I constantly kick them out of the kitchen and onto the dining room floor to serve.

I'm teaching a front of the house management and customer service credit course in a culinary program that serves meals during college luncheons. This is where I come to life. Teaching. Maybe I've finally found my niche. I'm at Kingsborough Community College in the Manhattan Beach section of Brooklyn. I teach customer service in catering and restaurant operations at their Tourism and Hospitality Culinary program.

Unbelievably, another few years have passed. It seems ages since I left Poland for the United States. My journey has taken all sorts of twists and turns as I try to find my calling. Not to mention, move up the social ladder. From babysitting and housekeeping to catering and tour guiding. It's been a bumpy road that leads me to this college instructor position. Is this my next stop on the journey or have I ultimately found my career?

How did I get this position at Kingsborough? It just happens. Serendipity, I suppose you'd call it. One day an opportunity opens for me when the previous instructor is laid off. But honestly, she wasn't the best teacher. Since I'm already working at the college as a lab technician, I take my chance and ask about the job opening. I get the nerve to talk to John, my dear friend and director of the culinary department.

John knows I have hands-on experience in catering service and that I'd be perfect for the position. He knows my strengths (and weaknesses!) and has always given me support and the chance to grow. John is my angel. I met him when I was still a student, so we have a long history. To my delight, John gives me the adjunct professor job.

•

Let's backpedal to the first time I met John. It's the first day of my first Customer Service class and I'm running late. Sweaty and breathless, I enter the classroom where John is teaching. Tall, bold, strong, he stands at the whiteboard explaining the importance of manners in the customer service trade. Without missing a beat, John begins, "Oh, and for example, someone is running late for their own party..." With a sardonic smile, he looks straight at me.

Chapter Ten - A College Career

Still out of breath, I can't respond yet. All I can do is smile back at him. John's sarcasm takes my confidence—and cockiness—away. I'm ready to learn—and will never be late again. I appreciate John's directness as well as his sense of humor. I like him right away.

I find a quiet spot in the back of the classroom and prepare to play hard ball with the instructor. I wait for the best moment for a comeback. John proceeds to give a long monologue on customer service. Preaching charismatically, he immediately reminds me of Martin Luther King, Jr. and his "I have a dream" speech. It's something about John's engagement, animation and passion. It's as if John knows the class strives to make our mark in the service industry but we're not quite there yet. Out of nowhere, I reply. "Said who, Martin Luther King?"

John immediately gets the reference and throws his marker at me. That's the beginning of our friendship. Even after my graduation, we stay friends. John suggests I work in Kingsborough's Culinary department as a kitchen lab technician. I do. Basically, I'm responsible for preparing food for cooking classes. Which means, I gather ingredients and control the food quality. I oversee the flow of food to the walk-in fridge and freezers, receiving and storing deliveries following New York State's strict food safety standards.

The kitchen lab tech job is a good fit for me. I already have experience in the food industry, mostly in the service arena, but I still need kitchen experience. I definitely get it at Kingsborough. My days are full of kitchen work. I really enjoy it and learn about the management side of the business.

Us lab technicians also assist professors. This is an ideal opportunity to improve our skills and learn from the best. I assist in the "Culinary One" course, which teaches the basics of cooking. Plus, I assist during a Food Improvisation class. In addition, I help during noncredit, continuing education classes for adults and disabled children. The work is varied, interesting and fulfilling. Kitchen lab techs are involved in various college projects. One of them is a pig testicles assignment. (Yes, I know, disgusting!) We are tasked with developing a recipe for a dish that incorporates pig testicles. The purpose? To reduce some of the food industry waste and use all parts of the animal. My suggestion: testicles dumplings.

Now, dumplings (or pierogis) are pretty much the national dish in Poland and have many different stuffings. I figure that chopped testicles can be one of the ingredients instead of regular meat. Mixed with mushrooms, the taste is very similar to beef.

My cooking partner is a student chef from Trinidad, amazed by pig testes. Kathleen thinks they're shaped like baby empanadas. There are a total of six techs recruited for this project. Some make Vietnamese-style buns stuffed with sliced testes meat while others make testicle sausage. Every dish is distinctive, reflecting our diverse cultural backgrounds.

To me, they all remind me of liver, which again, is a popular dish in Poland. I don't consider this a unique taste, but it's considered too exotic for the American palate. And for some in New York City, which has a large Muslim and Jewish population, pig testes are *verboten*. And definitely not kosher or halal.

I await the decision on which testes dish will be chosen.

•

The "pig testicle project" gives me an idea for a dumpling contest I organize and launch. It's the first big event I coordinate on my own. I feel so strongly about it that I believe it can become a yearly food fest in Manhattan—a city that loves its annual food festivals.

Unfortunately, my dumpling competition never gets off the ground. But through no fault of my own.

Just bad luck, I guess. Everything is well organized. I've secured the perfect venue, a popular East Village bar that hosts food pop-ups. Several restaurants have committed to entering dumplings in the competition. The plan is for customers to purchase tickets for an evening of dumplings, beer and fun. How can it fail?

My New York dumpling contest features entries in a variety of styles and flavors. Besides traditional Polish pierogi stuffed with cheese, cabbage or mushrooms there are Russian dumplings, stuffed with potatoes and vegan dumplings stuffed with a selection of veggies and tofu. The dumplings are either boiled or fried, served straight up or with toppings like sour cream and caramelized onions. A wide assortment of cuisines is featured. I'm so excited to organize an event that highlights the diverse culinary culture of New York City.

In this Manhattan melting pot, Polish (ish) foods like pretzels, borscht and pierogies are extremely popular in both the East Village and the Lower East Side. They have become part of the city's ethnic food heritage. At the beginning of 19th century, European immigrants flooded the Lower East Side and brought their culinary history with them. I notice a pierogies rebirth in the 21st century and want to capitalize on it. I try to accomplish this by promoting the dumpling competition with hipsters in the East Village and in Greenpoint's Polish community.

The night before the dumpling contest, I'm so excited, I can't sleep. I make sure everything's ready, but I still can't shake an unsettling feeling. Fear? Doubt? Something tells me it's not going to work. And it doesn't.

At the last minute, the bar hosting the event gets closed by the Department of Health. I don't know if this is just a coincidence or if someone unhappy with my dumpling contest called the Department of Health on the venue.

I still manage to make the event happen, though. I find an Egyptian restaurant nearby to host the event, but it just isn't the same. Many guests cancel and I have no choice but to return their money. The place isn't as popular as the original venue. It doesn't bring in a crowd. Most of the attendees are friends or friends of friends who come by to give me support. The dumpling competition is a testament to friendship rather than a bona-fide food contest. I end up losing big time.

Afterwards, I believe even more in the power of friendship, but I stop believing in myself. I kick all my ideas and my potential projects to the curb. This failed event puts me off for the next few years. I don't want to organize anything and have strong doubts about both my organizational skills and my judgement. Like a popped balloon, I feel as though I've lost all my oxygen. My American Dream is dead.

•

With my head between my legs in shame, I go back to my college testicles project. And yes, I even fail at this; my recipe idea is also turned down. The consensus is that the taste is unpleasant. Ultimately, nobody is interested in saving pig testicles for future processing into Polish dumplings. I guess New Yorkers still prefer the processed meat flavor of hot dogs boiled in greasy water which are sold from carts all over the city. These "dirty water dogs" have become a symbol of New York.

I continue working in the Kingsborough College kitchen as a lab tech, assisting in classes and brainstorming on food-related projects. Besides my college job, I'm still catering and serving at parties all around the city. I've gained useful experience in service, management and food safety and am now ready to share my knowledge with others. This is when opportunity knocks and John needs a new "front of the house" instructor. I know I'm perfect for this position; it feels

Chapter Ten - A College Career

tailor-made for me. John feels the same way and offers me the gig.

And it *is* perfect...except for having to say, "Serve from the left, clean from the right" over and over again to my students. Will they ever get the hang of it?

The sound of breaking glass sound demands my attention. Damn, this is what happens when students refuse to learn this one simple—important!—rule. They're more interested in learning how to cook, not serve. They don't grasp that knowing a little bit about all aspects of the hospitality trade is key to their future careers. I totally get it—cooking is more pleasurable and more creative than serving. But knowing another skill is important too.

In my free time, I enroll in culinary courses so I can get access to the college kitchens. By taking these classes, I expand my knowledge and become a better teacher. When I do catering gigs, I try to get involved in kitchen prep. Increasing my learning curve can only help my career.

John knows I'm extremely interested in cooking professionally. This is why he recommends me to Kingsborough's Continuing Education Department to teach additional culinary classes. In one, I show kids kitchen skills and in another, I teach adults how to make *tapas*. Although I love leading both classes, I still feel something's missing. I want more! But more of what, I just don't know.

After I'm done teaching one day, I decide to stop by John's office. He always gives me such good advice and I love picking his brain. Nervously, I check my watch, hoping my students clean up fast and leave the classroom. I pack my books quickly, but I end up making a mess. Papers fly all over my desk. I grab them haphazardly, mixing up the order. All I want is to get to John's before he leaves for the day. For some reason, seeing him feels urgent.

Lights off, door locked, I run down the hall. "Are you chasing someone?" a warm voice asks. John!

"Yes, mostly myself," I tell him. "But this time, it's you!" Out of breath, I tell John, "I wanted to make it to your office before you left."

"Well, you caught me," he laughs. "Let's go back inside so we can talk."

I explain to my mentor that I'm tired of just teaching about the food service industry. I want to do something more creative and inspiring, something cooking related. But I'm not sure what.

John smiles. "Here's your chance," he begins. "I'm working on a book about weird foods around the world. If you'd like to contribute a chapter, it's yours. Just pick one." He hands me a bunch of pages stapled together. Listed are unusual dishes people eat across the globe. I scan the entries quickly. Some have names handwritten beside them, but others are blank. Those chapters are still available. The book will be called *They Eat That?: A Cultural Encyclopedia of Weird and Exotic Food from around the World.* I'm lucky to be part of it.

One entry jumps out at me. Human placenta. Ugh. This immediately has no appeal. Rats are also listed. I might just puke. Not only is it gross but I feel so sorry for the helpless animals people eat around the world. I'm not sure if I want to contribute to this encyclopedia of horrors, but on the other hand it's an opportunity for recognition. Contributing to a book will look impressive on my resume. Is this what I've been looking for?

After all, celebrity chef and author Anthony Bourdain travels the planet eating bizarre local entrees. He even has a TV show as well as books on the market. And as far as I know, though, no one's written a book about weird foods yet. Maybe I've found my niche.

Flipping through the pages John has given me, something catches my eye: a chapter on lizard soup. *Hmm,* I think, *I can make this without causing too much harm to nature. I can sacrifice one, maybe two lizards,* I convince myself. I scribble my name next to the lizard

Chapter Ten - A College Career

chapter and hand the papers back to John. He reads my choice and nods approvingly, "Okay," he tells me. "You have one month to do it."

I toss and turn that night. *Where the heck am I going to get a lizard in Brooklyn? A pet store? And how do you kill—and gut—a lizard?* I can't sleep. My head is full of reptilian thoughts. I'm scared I signed myself up for too big of a challenge. Bigger than myself.

First of all, I've never prepped and cooked anything as bizarre as a lizard. And I thought the testicle project was weird! In comparison, it was easier and less outlandish than this one. Second, since English is not my native tongue, how am I going to write a whole chapter—and recipe—about lizard soup?

On top of everything, I consider lizards my friends! How can I cook and eat a friend? Since childhood, I always had a special relationship with lizards. Growing up in the mountains of Poland, lizards were plentiful. Newts, salamanders and other creatures. (Okay, so they're technically amphibians, but still...) Seeing their cute, little bodies sunbathing on a rock or skittering on the ground thrilled me. They ran so effortlessly, so quickly. I was amazed at how their colors adjusted to their environment. They seemed sleepy but wide awake at the same time. Plus, they could lose their tails and still survive without them.

Lizards are my tiny superheroes, my spirit animals. I think of them as I struggle to acclimate to life in New York City. I aspire to be like them, adjustable, adaptable, always on the alert and ready to go. I even have a tattoo of a lizard on my ankle. So, how can I cook—and eat!—my hero, my inspiration, my soul animal and best friend? It's a huge dilemma.

I wake up the next day, surprisingly clearheaded. I know exactly what to do. I need to push my reluctance aside and make the damn soup. I need to let my spirit animal help me succeed as a chef. I can't pass up this unique opportunity to contribute a chapter to this book. But how do I find a lizard in the city? I bet my friend Jasmine, who's Chinese, will know. When I call Jasmine, she agrees to meet me for a "lizard hunt." She sounds excited by the challenge. "Maggie, I'll meet you in Chinatown in two hours," she says.

I touch my lizard tattoo for good luck—and maybe for its blessing. "We're going to do it just this once," I promise. "For a greater purpose." But I still feel conflicted inside. *What we won't do for fame and fortune,* I sigh to myself.

The Q train deposits me on Canal Street in Manhattan, a stop that's always busy, no matter the time of day or day of the week. The station is so crowded I have to push my way through the bodies to get up the stairs and onto the street. There's a smile on Jasmine's face when she sees me. She wears a pair of fancy glasses and is sporting a designer bag, Gucci maybe. Man, she looks very classy. Slightly overdressed to go lizard-shopping in Chinatown, I think. But I'm glad she's agreed to help me on my quest.

The pungent odor of the Chinese market immediately hits me. Fish of almost every variety sit in boxes of ice that bleed onto the sidewalk. The Chinatown streets are loud and stinky. Besides the fish, fruit and vegetables, a selection of bootleg designer wristwatches and handbags are available. Knockoffs of Gucci and Louis Vuitton. The items are fake and illegal but easily accessible in Chinatown. You can get anything you need here—even a lizard. You just have to know the right person to help you get it.

With Jasmine, the whole reptile-shopping experience is much easier. She's not a stranger to these streets, not a tourist, and she speaks the language. Jasmine knows what she wants and where to find it. She takes me into a store crammed with unusual-looking herbs, spices, deer antlers and other hard-to-describe goods. I don't know what half of them are!

Chapter Ten - A College Career

From one of the shelves, she pulls out a bag with a dried gecko in it. Just like that! "Here you go, Maggie," she says. "For your soup."

I can't believe it. As I take a closer look, I notice other dead creatures on that out-of-the-way shelf. Lizards, reptiles and warm-blooded animals too. Do people really eat them? These cute, vulnerable things? I push away the dried gecko. This is horrible!

I'm reminded of the time I ate alligator and frog. To me, they taste almost the same, but alligators are gamier. People try to make themselves feel less guilty for eating them by saying that they taste just like chicken. I admit, they do taste similar, but...

However, the excitement of having my essay in a book kills any doubts—or food guilt. I'm happy to explore the intricacies of lizard soup just to get published. Hopefully, lizard will remind me of chicken too. And I'm glad we found the gecko. Jasmine and I celebrate with Chinese sweets at one of the many bakeries here.

•

My very generous boss, who's in charge of the kitchens at Kingsborough, allows me to use the facilities after hours to create my lizard concoction. After researching similar soups (like alligator), I decide to make two different versions of lizard soup. One is more traditional and reminds me of Grandma's chicken soup. The other is more Asian with a coconut cream base.

Besides crafting the soup, I still need to write a chapter on it. I have to tell in what culture it's popular and why. For the chapter to be complete, I need to pinpoint what part of the world it's from and explain how to prepare the dish. Luckily, I get plenty of support from my friends and coworkers. They are happy to taste my soup and give me advice. By some miracle, I make my publishing deadline and hand in my lizard soup chapter.

My greatest surprise comes from my vegan friend Iris. She decides to accompany me to the New York Public Library book launch of *They Eat That?...* Iris knows she'll be exposed to a subject she strongly opposes. There's a slew of unusual dishes in the encyclopedia and most of them are animal-based. Despite all this, Iris still wants to go with me. I guess she knows how important the book is to me. "This time, I'll come to celebrate your achievement in violence," she lectures. "But the next time, you'll contribute to a book on veganism. And I'll be there too. You'll see, Maggie!" For good measure, Iris adds, "Your sins will be forgiven."

I don't know what vegan future Iris is talking about but I'm happy to have her by my side to celebrate my carnivorous achievement. *I made it,* I tell myself. *I contributed to a book! My name is published in a book!*

It finally feels like my American Dream is within reach.

Chapter Eleven
Behind My American Dream

In the years that follow, I stop working catering jobs and put my full focus on teaching customer service and cooking classes. Besides that, I teach Introduction to Tourism and still take private groups throughout the East Coast on weekends. I'm right out there on the stage nonstop, either lecturing or touring. My efforts—and skills—have been recognized and I've gotten more job offers. Some I accept, some I don't. For me, a job being a good fit with my personality is crucial.

I'm told about an adjunct professor position at SUNY's Brooklyn Educational Opportunity Center (BEOC) in Tourism and Hospitality. (SUNY stands for State University of New York and is the largest comprehensive university system in the United States.) I'm recommended for the position by a friend from Kingsborough Community College. The interview goes well and I get the job. I'm living my dream! I do what I love and get more and more opportunities because of my hard work and dedication. The adjunct professor position is more than I hoped for. I look forward to my first day at work.

When I walk into my classroom on the City Tech campus in Downtown Brooklyn, I immediately notice that my students are of different ages and ethnicities. It's a true New York City fusion—of which this Polish girl is a part. Best of all, their education is tuition-free.

My students are mostly African American but there are a fair share of Asians and Latinos. They're not much older than I am. Many have been laid off and are looking to learn new skills that will lead to other job opportunities—and certification credentials.

I can see by their faces that some are disappointed and frustrated with life, while others look full of hope. As I quickly scan my students, they check me out too, probably wondering who I am and what I can do for them. There are about 15 in all. The silent question passes between us: "How did this immigrant chick get this job?"

For a minute, I feel their unspoken judgement and don't know where to begin. I take a deep breath and decide to be honest with them about where I've been and what I've done, what's led me to this moment. I start with my ethnic background. I'm truthful about how hard it is to start from scratch in an unfamiliar place in an unfamiliar tongue. Their faces soften. Maybe speaking from my heart has touched theirs. I tell a story that's familiar—difficulty with a new language, with a new country, the homesickness, the struggle.

When I finish my intro, I hope they can see how similar I am to them—searching for a place in a society that's dominated by white men. They seem to get it. My heartfelt talk helps them see my humanity. I feel a bond between us. I'm glad we connect but sad at the same time. Why? Because it poses a question: Is the American Dream available to all of us no matter who or what you are?

This question plagues me during my early months of teaching at SUNY BEOC. I learn a lot from my students. I dive deep into racism and the lack of equal rights in American society. I touch upon important topics, but I

Chapter Eleven - Behind My American Dream

still feel disappointed. I'm tired of seeing the white race succeed while others struggle because of prejudice.

My perspective on many things has changed since the day I started teaching at BEOC. My idea of the American Dream has gotten twisted. It's not the same anymore. I question everything I do; much of it doesn't make sense anymore. It's not what I imagined a decade ago. I feel I'm hunting something I can never reach.

Yes, as an adjunct professor, I have a position in society, but it doesn't seem to matter. I still struggle supporting myself financially. All my jobs are part-time. Making a living in the city is tough. Part-time work doesn't guarantee stability. I don't have health benefits. I don't have paid vacation time. I don't have job security—I can be fired from any of my jobs at any time. The race for my American Dream is exhausting!

Although I work my ass off, I still don't earn enough money. And it's not just me who has to juggle several jobs at the same time; it's a New York City phenomenon. The cost of living is high and it's so crowded. Sometimes I feel like there's no space to breathe. You work. And you party to forget how hard you work. Then you do it again the next day. There's no room for downtime. You keep running toward something. But what? There's no end to this vicious cycle. So, I'm the one who has to end it. I think my students help me realize this.

Somewhere along the road, my American Dream has become deformed. This is not the career I was hoping for. I question who am and what I want to do the rest of my life. I feel confused, conflicted. Recently, I've been wondering if there's something more for me out there and what's really behind my American Dream. I do a ton of soul-searching and come up empty.

The truth is, I'm tired of serving at events. (Yes, I started doing them again to make ends meet.) It's not lively and fun anymore. That's one of the reasons I want to stop doing catering jobs. They're loud, exhausting drunkfests. It's the same thing over and over again. Only the location and the people change. The rest is interchangeable. Attitude, alcohol, blaring music, hours of working on your feet. It's not for me anymore. Too much intense physical labor.

I feel the same about being a tour guide. It's hours of walking, often in horrible weather. I visit the same places, tell the same stories, just to different groups. Sometimes I long to be on the other side of the equation: being taken around a city like a VIP. But in this city? Maybe I'm just tired of New York.

Even my adjunct teaching position doesn't appeal to me anymore. Semester after semester, I repeat myself, but to a new crowd of students. Am I actually helping them by preparing them for jobs in a difficult field? I'm not learning anything new; I'm not growing. I feel stuck. Burned out.

Statistically speaking, an individual changes their career three to seven times in their lifetime. In my life, it feels like I constantly need to adapt to a new location, to a new marketplace. Just to keep from being bored. Is there something wrong with me?

I've come to believe that the American Dream is just a fantasy in the toughest reality. You need to spend your entire life busting your ass to chase your goal. Or get lucky. Yes, anything could happen in the States—but only if luck is on your side. If not, then you're just wasting your time. The cult of work in the US and the "it's not what you know but who you know" system of getting ahead doesn't allow space for anything else. When did I get so jaded?

I miss Europe with its long vacations, flexible work schedules and better social services—universal healthcare, for one. And it's not just me who realizes this. More and more Americans are moving to southern Europe. Places like Spain, Portugal and Greece. The cost of living is cheaper. The lunch breaks are longer and perks like paid family leave are the norm. There's something to be said for a better quality of life.

I want changes too. I want to escape from New York. Before this realization, it felt like I could achieve anything I wanted. My American Dream was an inspiration. But now it has become an illusion. A fantasy. What was I looking for here in Dreamland anyway?

Chapter Twelve
What's Cooking?

My love for food and the kitchen environment grows the more I work as a server. I love being in a professional kitchen; it's full of action and excitement. Both the United Nations and Tavern on The Green have large events with many prepping and cooking stations. Every chef and cook works separately and is responsible for their own dish or dishes. For example, there's a soup station, a salad station, even a cook who only makes sauces. Like the links in a chain, all these little jobs mesh to contribute to the success of the event.

The warmth of the kitchen and its symphony of smells is enticing. It puts out a rich variety of dishes and that are all perfectly assembled. Plate presentation is an art in itself. I want to be part of that kitchen magic. Being a server doesn't have the same allure.

These exclusive, private events work like a well-oiled machine. Loads of people are hired to do specific tasks—and this is behind the scenes before a plate even leaves the kitchen. I remember at one event, two young Israeli guys were hired just to decorate the plates and platters. They used all sorts of natural plants like herbs, edible flowers, fresh chives and even moss. Their plates were an incredible sight. Another fellow was hired just to taste the food before it left the kitchen. And these "specialty" workers didn't include the chefs who put together the dishes. The guests never see these people, yet they enjoy their delicious creations.

I'm fascinated by the way a commercial kitchen works. I already have experience in college kitchens and teaching basic cooking classes, but that's not the same thing. My knowledge is nothing compared to the synchronicity of a working restaurant kitchen. And I'm stoked to learn more.

Teaching front of the house service or tourism is nowhere near as riveting as being part of the back of the house—the kitchen. That's where I want to shift my focus. But how?

I decide to quit my job at Kingsborough I need to take a break from tour guiding too. I keep rejecting calls about server gigs from catering companies. I feel a change coming. But I want to *be* the change. I'm aware that nobody will hire me in a New York commercial kitchen without hands-on restaurant experience, so I need to find another way to get there. And for me, it's always a crooked path. In a roundabout way, I find it in yoga.

•

I'd recently gotten into yoga and practice regularly at a local studio. I'm intrigued when the studio offers a three-month yoga retreat in the Bahamas. With a few hours of volunteer work each day, you can attend the retreat free of charge. They call it karma yoga—you give your time; they give you room and board. One of the options is working in the kitchen.

I can't get the yoga retreat out of my mind. I can flee the cold, gray New York winter and escape to warm, exotic Paradise Island. While I'm there, I can plan my next move plus get cooking experience in the ashram kitchen. I can use this knowledge as a jumping off point and see where it takes me. I decide to go for it!

In the Bahamas, there are five of us helpers, a karma yogi plus a chef who is also a yoga instructor. Each day, we prepare meals for about 300 people. Christmas is the busiest season at the ashram. Starting in the afternoon, we work five to six hours a day to make the evening meal. The philosophy behind food at the ashram is to make enough vegetarian or vegan food for all and to simply follow the yogi diet. With the yogi diet comes the belief in *ahimsa,* which is nonviolence. The food we eat is mostly fresh fruits and vegetables. No meat products.

We start and end the day with yoga and meditation. Cooking begins with a yogic prayer to create positive energy in the kitchen. Yogis believe that meals should be prepped with the bare hands because they're an extension of your "naked soul." This way, you send energy into the food with your touch, your essence. No gloves, just hands. This follows the yogic belief that we transmit our love and life force energy (or *prana*) into food.

After the prayer ceremony, we transition to prepping. In a vegetarian kitchen, this means lots of veggies. We do nothing but chop for the next two or more hours. When all the ingredients are ready, then we focus on cooking. We combine all the necessary ingredients to create a healthy, flavorful dish.

The five yogi kitchen workers toil hard in the tiny space. All the equipment is antiquated and there's no air-conditioner, just an ancient fan. It's hot in the Bahamas and the ashram kitchen is not well laid out for the climate. There's little ventilation, and in terms of heat, the temperature is comparable to any busy New York restaurant kitchen.

Although my hands and arms are decorated with cuts and burns, I like what I do. I enjoy getting my hands dirty. I love the feeling of different textures against my skin—

smooth, silky, chunky, firm. I enjoy the meditative trance I enter while chopping. This is when I can finally focus on my mantras. (Mantras are words or phrases you repeat in your mind to aid concentration during meditation.) I'm excited about learning new skills that I hope will improve my health and my life in general.

Volunteering in the ashram kitchen confirms my desire to shift my career focus from front of the house to back of the house. It appears that food likes me too because I have a knack for turning out nice dishes. It gives me a feeling of completion, of accomplishment. Even though I'm exhausted at the end of the day, I feel satisfied and content.

I expand my nutrition horizons at the ashram. And not just with vegetarian food, but vegan too. As a lover of animals, for a long time I've considered giving up eating animal products, but I honestly didn't know how. Well, the ashram kitchen is teaching me. I feel veganism could be an alternate life path.

After my three-month stint at the ashram is over and I must return to the real world, I decide that I need (deserve!) to be in a quiet place and work in a healthy environment. City or country? It doesn't matter. But wherever I end up, I picture myself both in a vegan kitchen and as a yoga instructor. That's my future. That's my new dream.

For now, I'm enjoying working in the ashram kitchen, living at a beautiful beach, basking in the sun surrounded by (mostly) kind people. The relaxed ambiance is accompanied by a solid plan that plays in my head like a mantra: "Follow your new dreams—vegan food and a yogi lifestyle." I do just that.

But there are challenges. "Cut the tofu into thinner slices!" my boss Pranava squawks at me. "They're too big." Everything I do at the beginning of my kitchen experience, is wrong. But Pranava is this way with all of us. He's a perfectionist, and a kid sole at the time time

Chapter Twelve - What's Cooking?

but firm. Although I hate to admit it, I still learn from Pranava, despite his brashness sometime. I cherish my time there. Three months pass in the blink of an eye.

Before I know it, I'm back in the continental US, back to reality. This time, my reality is in New Jersey. Soon after I return, I find a job in a vegan restaurant in the Garden State. I miss ashram life and Paradise Island, though. My memories are still vivid. I miss the beach, my yogi friends and the (mostly) peaceful kitchen.

I meet my new partner soon after my return to the States and through her, get connected to the owners of VeganV. I'm hired for a sous chef position. Along with the title comes the responsibility of preparing food, cooking it and getting it out there to be served. I'm responsible for stocking the pantry and refrigerators and seeing that our food is fresh and up-to-date. The offerings at VeganV are organic and gluten-free which requires special care. But I'm up for the task.

I start early in the morning by opening the restaurant. I'm the only one there for the first few hours. Working solo, I move fast prepping for the day. I enjoy being alone. It's quiet and meditative. I accomplish all the chopping by playing silent mantras in my head, just like we did at the ashram. Right before noon, the introspective atmosphere changes as the front and back of the house staff arrive. But by then, I'm ready for company.

VeganV is a small café owned by a female couple and operated by a small team of workers, all women. Besides myself, there's one other member of the kitchen staff. Lana's tasked with making sweets and working on the line during dinner service. I do the lunch line service by myself. There's one dishwasher who helps during the rush, and two, sometimes three, waitresses. At noon, we all move fast, including the dinner chef who arrives around then.

It's the owner, Flora, who I adore. We understand each other. I appreciate the connection and chats we have while working. I learn tons from Flora about the vegan diet. I learn how to use plant protein products like seitan, tofu and several others I've never used before. I learn all about the vegan world. That's the main reason I'm here. To learn.

I still need to know a lot more about veganism—i.e., how to substitute one product for another to mimic the taste of meat or cheese, foods that have similar textures to the originals. I learn how to make plant-based cheese and other items. I also contribute my own specialties to the menu—items like borscht soup and baba ghanoush. People love them. I feel I'm on a new path to the American Dream. This time, in the vegan kitchen.

•

"I cut it exactly the way you showed me the last time, chef! The avocado looks exactly like yours, CHEF!" This is my mean side responding to Chef Sam's criticism. Although it's been few years since I started working at VeganV, the same conflict arises. But as angry as you are at a coworker, there's this tried-and-true kitchen rule just as there is in most bustling, New York City kitchens: it is to always say the word "chef" at the end of a statement when you're addressing your boss. It feels like the military, true, but it's supposed to be "Yes, chef!" and "No, chef!" no matter what. It's a sign of respect. I guess everyone needs a title and a position on the culinary ladder.

A professional kitchen can be a volatile place. Even a vegan kitchen. It feels like a fight is about to erupt. Chef Sam doesn't like something I do. Yet again. The last time, it was the way I was plating up salad. This time, I'm serving too much chili even though it's exactly the same amount she showed me before. Jeez, Chef Sam is yelling at me again. We may need to move our conflict outside, away from the customers' eyes.

Chapter Twelve - What's Cooking?

This won't be the first time Chef Sam and I have had a fist fight. But I don't feel like taking it to the street today, so I try my best to hold my temper. However, I won't allow anyone to talk down to me. Especially not in front of my colleagues and the customers. Yogi Maggie thinks it's so fucking *not* namaste. Yogi Maggie is losing her patience.

And it's not just me who complains about Chef Sam. Everyone does. But it still doesn't help my wounded ego that I'm not the only one she digs into. I just don't need negativity in my life. As much as I love VeganV and the other chef, sometimes I wonder if I should leave. My dream is still to become a vegan chef one day. Just not in this kind of environment. It's so ironic—the food is "clean" in VeganV but the work setting is toxic.

Although I enjoy my work, the salary is low. Kitchen jobs are one of the lowest paying careers in the United States. In truth, there aren't many positions in the food service industry that pay well. To make the big bucks, either you have to become a celebrity chef or you open your own business. But neither guarantee success. Sixty percent of restaurants fail within the first year, 80% before the first five years. Rents are astronomical, and so is the cost of running the operation. It's a lose-lose situation.

Adding to my disillusion is the fact that I'm ready to move somewhere warmer. Like California. I've always dreamed of living there. I take the Natalie Merchant song "San Andreas Fault" to heart. The lyrics play over and over in my head:

"Go west / Paradise is there. / You'll have all that you can eat. / Of milk & honey over there. / You'll be the brightest star / the world has ever seen..."

Those words are a mantra in my head 24/7. The idea grows on me and I start directing my life toward the big move and my next transformation. I go west.

Chapter Thirteen
New Dream, New Destination

"Turn off the red switch at the bottom!" someone yells at me. Although it snaps me awake, it takes me a few seconds to realize where I am. I manage to find the switch on the empanada machine. As fast as I can, I reach the emergency button and the belt stops moving with a loud snap.

Everybody's eyes are on me. I feel so embarrassed but on the other hand, I can't stop laughing on the inside when I look down at the empanadas smashed together on the machine's belt. I feel like Ethel in the "I Love Lucy" episode that takes place in the chocolate factory. Lucy and Ethel battled the machine too.

Covering my mouth with my hand, I run to the bathroom to escape my coworkers' critical gaze. Once in the stall, I laugh out loud. I laugh so hard that tears run down my cheeks. I can't stop giggling no matter what I do. My whole body responds to my laughter. I start sweating profusely, shaking. I desperately need fresh air but there's no window to open; there are no windows anywhere in the factory.

That's right, I fulfilled my dream to come to sunny California, but I'm stuck in a windowless factory. Plus, my training is not going too smoothly. What the heck am I doing here? I know this job is not for me even though it promises good money and good benefits. Although the position of shift leader sounds interesting, the reality is not. In fact, it sucks.

A few weeks earlier, I found an ad online for Amy's Kitchen, the vegetarian/vegan producer of healthy food. You know the Amy's—their frozen dinners and pizzas fill grocery stores across America. Well, the ad stated that Amy's is looking for a leaders to help runing their pizza factory that will soon open in San Jose, California. The position's title is Production Line Leader. I'd be in charge of overseeing employees and, as the name implies, I'd also be responsible for the product production line.

At first, I get excited. I already have leadership experience and have worked with vegan food before. Since moving to San Jose a year earlier, I've worked in a vegan restaurant as a shift leader. I really like that place and my boss but not the money. Again, I make too little to survive, especially on the West Coast.

Amy's Kitchen, on the other hand, is steady work with a strong salary and benefits package. I decide to take the job when it's offered. Before I start, all I have to do is complete training in their factory, which is located near the Napa Valley, two hours away from where I live. They pay for my accommodations and gas plus give me a salary during my training period. It's a no brainer. I pack my bag and drive toward my bright, shiny future.

The first day of training is just safety lectures and going over rules and regs. The orientation includes a history of the Amy's Kitchen family business. I find it quite interesting. The rest of my day consists of food safety guidelines as well as machine operations. After hours of lectures, I'm treated to an excellent lunch, which, to my surprise is absolutely not vegan. After few more

Chapter Thirteen - New Dream, New Destination

hours of training, we end the day. I'm excited for what tomorrow will bring because Day One is pretty easy. I go to my cushy hotel room to catch some sleep.

Day Two of training finds me donning a uniform, plastic slippers and earplugs before stepping onto Amy's factory floor. Everything must be completely sanitary in the prep area. My plastic shoes are washed before I leave the dressing room. The cleaning job is performed by a special device that brushes your feet as you pass through the door.

I step onto the cavernous factory floor that's filled with machines. The space is divided into stations that make various products. Each has a different function. For example, there's one to make tofu, a contraption I've never seen in my life—even though I've cooked with tofu extensively. I'm amazed by all the equipment.

Employees wear uniforms in a dull rainbow of colors to signify the section where they work. I learn that you're not allowed to walk freely into another section without a supervisor's approval. Everything is controlled by team leaders and supervisors. I've never been in a place like this before. It's fascinating.

Dressed in a blue uniform, I'm overseeing empanada production on my second day of training. For eight hours, workers are posted at their production line, mine being the empanada apparatus. Approximately 10 people are gathered around the machine, folding empanadas. Then the machine shoots each turnover onto the belt. Sometimes it jams, so it needs to be unjammed. Which is my task for the day: empanada overseer.

I don't know what happened. Maybe the monotony of staring at the marching empanadas lulls me into a trance or I drift off to sleep. But the last thing remember is hearing, "Switch off the machine!" before running into the ladies' room. Now, I'm sitting on the toilet, still laughing hysterically, wondering how this story will end. Something tells me I'll get my answer soon.

I desperately need fresh air. There's none in the restroom or in the stagnant factory. I need to go outside. I pass a dining hall where some workers are already on break. They're having a good time, chatting with each other, laughing, joking around. Maybe I should take my break now too since I'm already there.

The cafeteria is filled with tables and there are also picnic benches outdoors. The people sitting at them speak mostly Spanish, which I don't understand. But still, they're friendly. With gestures, they invite me to join them.

Those who speak English interact with me. Everyone is super nice and I enjoy their positive vibes. I learn more about their lives, inside and outside of Amy's Kitchen. Most have worked here for 20 years or more. Much longer than my entire time in the US. After decades of dedication and hard work, they have longer vacation time and better benefits. Amy's makes an effort to ensure that their employees are content. There are so many horror stories about escapes from horrible lives in their homelands—like Mexico, Columbia and Guatemala. After getting their Green Cards, they found job stability at Amy's and have everything they need.

This all sounds wonderful. But as friendly as they are and as good an employer as Amy's is, I know I don't fit in here. Maybe this place is *their* American Dream, but it's not mine. Watching pizzas and empanadas parade down a conveyer belt, making sure that everything and everyone works smoothly is my idea of hell. Eight hours a day, five days a week in a stifling factory without sunlight doesn't sound healthy—or appealing. Constant exposure to cold and the loud noise generated by the machines is another horror. I wasn't meant to be part of this. Even in such a welcoming atmosphere, the work conditions themselves are hostile. After two days of training, I decide to leave.

Amy's Kitchen still pays me for the entire week even though I only work two days, which is generous of them.

Chapter Thirteen - New Dream, New Destination

It gives me a little financial cushion but I know that I have to immediately return to my job search.

This time, I look for a position in my field: veganism, yoga or front of the house management. My choices are extremely limited. There are only a handful of vegan options here. I apply to several types: restaurants, college cafeterias, cafés. I hope to get a job soon because my money won't last long.

Again, I begin to doubt my career choice. I'm not sure what my American Dream is anymore. Do I even have one at all? Besides just surviving? Maybe I should stop dreaming big. My personal achievements are not my goals anymore. My motivation has shifted to focusing on doing something to benefit the planet. That's my bigger picture.

It feels like I'm spinning aimlessly, repeating the same mistakes. I need a steady job but on the other hand, I don't enjoy the boredom of stability. I want to be independent, take risks. But I'm also afraid of risks. I resist jumping in with both feet, saying, "To hell with it!" and just going for it. Whatever "it" is. For weeks, I flounder.

•

When UC Davis calls me for an interview, I choose stability. The position is for dining room senior staff at the UC Davis dining hall. That's the only job currently available but I hope more opportunities will present themselves once my foot's in the door.

I'm so excited to be called that I don't even give the job specs a close look. My goal is just to get into the UC Davis system, even if it's menial work, get trained and learn of other jobs at the college. Who knows, in time, maybe they'll need a vegan chef or front of the house manager, positions that fit me better.

What I do remember about the job description is that the work conditions and starting salary are all right. In the meantime, I can look for something else in case this doesn't work out. But for now, I just want to get into UC Davis.

When Interview Day comes, it goes smoothly. They ask simple interview questions about food safety and customer service. So simple, I laugh to myself. I know I'm overqualified for the position, but an unnamed, invisible power tells me to take it if they offer it. And I have a feeling I'll get the job. (PS, I do.)

UC Davis is a well-respected university and one of ten campuses in the University of California system. As the name implies, it's located in Davis, an adorable town near Sacramento, the state capital. The campus is quite large, about 5,300 acres, and more than 31,000 students are enrolled. The main campus houses about 1,200 buildings, including various departments, libraries and student dorms. It's a small city.

The UC Davis campus itself doesn't steal my heart. The buildings are ultra-modern with no personality. Nothing special. Lots of cement and unimaginative architecture. There are no old shops like those you see around New York University, for example. At first glance, the UC Davis campus appears cold. But it's filled with interesting, young people. Its creative, youthful energy is undeniable. I feel it just by walking around the campus.

It makes me think back to when I was working as an adjunct instructor at Kingsborough Community College. But the difference is that Kingsborough is in a picturesque setting, facing the ocean. At UC Davis, you're surrounded by empty fields. (It started as an agricultural college back in 1905.) But compared to Kingsborough, the UC Davis students are more vibrant. Another difference between the two schools is that I'm at UC Davis not to teach but to serve in the dining room. I'm still not exactly sure what my role will be, but I'll learn soon.

Chapter Thirteen - New Dream, New Destination

When I arrive for my first day on the job, my manager gives me a tour of the dining room. Dave is over forty, tall and lean with gray hair. He seems cool, especially when he tries to calm me down after I announce that I'm overqualified for the position. "Maggie, chill and just wait," he tells me. "I'm sure you'll find something more suited to your skills set here. There are a bunch of food stations and job titles. Openings come up often. But everything takes time, just wait. Okay?"

"Okay," I tell him, breathing a sigh of relief. Dave continues, "But for now, you're at the beverage station."

"At the what?" I almost scream. I can't believe it! With my experience, they want me to watch coffee! Seriously?

I want to leave immediately but something tells me to stay. At least for a few days to see if anything changes. With that decision, I shadow Dave, my supervisor, learning my way around the dining room. My beverage station includes coffee, juices, teas and the soft drink machines which are located in different parts of the dining room. They're all under my care.

My duties include changing boxes at the soda wall which is situated at the back of the kitchen. I've never seen such a thing and it makes quite an impression on me. The soda station consists of a huge wall rack which holds gallons of soda boxes. They're attached to a carbonizer by pipes. (A carbonizer gives soft drinks bubbles.) After the soda is carbonized, it travels in underground pipes to the soda machines located all over the dining room. The soda boxes are extremely heavy and it's tough to change them single-handedly. "But you can always ask for help," Dave says. "If you can find someone. Everyone here is great."

Dave continues to show me around the kitchen and dining room food stations. I'm glad to see that one post features exclusively vegan foods. Other stations include vegan choices as well. Dave tells me that sometimes they'll need my help at the food stations as a server. I'm fine with that. Actually, I prefer it to watching coffee dispensers my entire workday. "Of course, you can count on me," I say to Dave, smiling.

He informs me that I'll close down the beverage station at 10 each night. This means I need to clean all the coffee machines and soda machines. This is the most time-consuming task of my entire day. The rest of my shift, I circulate through the dining room, checking soda stations and making coffee. It takes minutes to complete a rotation, so the rest of the time I just stand and watch the students enjoying their meals.

The food they serve at UC Davis is surprisingly tasty. Which is even more impressive because of the sheer number of people they serve—a minimum of 2,000 students daily. Obviously, it's not fine dining but it's unexpectedly good. And this isn't the only student dining room here; there are two more located in other parts of the campus. The quality and options, produced in massive quantities, are excellent.

Many products they use are prepacked to make food prep faster and easier and safer. I observe the kitchen operation during my lunch breaks or visits to the back of the house. I use my spare time to learn about new vegan options at the salad bar. I taste them and improve upon them—but only in my head. Sometimes I suggest other possible vegan dishes with the chefs, who are super nice and easy to talk to.

By now, they know I'm a vegan chef. They keep asking why I haven't applied for the cook position that's just become available. But the truth is, that job requires you to prepare whatever needs to be prepared, including meat products. With a smile, I respond, "I'd happy to but only if it's vegan."

•

It's been a month since I started at the UC Davis dining room. I help serve at different food stations, and forever

Chapter Thirteen - New Dream, New Destination

watch the coffee, which is my main task. Just to make sure I'm not bored, they add covering two water stations to my duties. Refilling water during dinner hours, which is their busiest time, keeps me running. I like the fast pace of the dinner rush because time goes faster. I'm also trained to work the cash register, which adds to my daily monotony.

I receive a phone call from Human Resources regarding the cook position, which I finally decide to apply for. Very politely, I explain that I'm vegan and I'm not sure if the job will guarantee that I will stay away from meat. One of the chefs told me that they prepare all the foods together, even vegan options. I inform HR that there's another position I applied for which I'm more interested in—a front of the house manager spot. I'm still waiting for a response about that one. I know US Davis needs more managers and I'm ready to step up. It looks like my supervisors will give me the thumbs up. Dave offers his help to prepare me for the interview, which I hope will happen soon. My other supervisors say they'd be happy to answer any questions I might have.

Overall, the managers at UC Davis are terrific and so is the whole kitchen crew. I make friends with my coworkers, who are diverse in age and ethnicity. Grad students and those over 50 work together seamlessly. Black, white, Asian, Latino...people from all over the globe work together in the kitchen or the front of the house work in harmony. It's kind of beautiful.

Some have been at UC Davis for as long as 20 years and are waiting to retire—the school offers an excellent pension plan. Others stay for the stability of the job, the great work atmosphere and solid health benefits. All of the above are necessary in the ridiculously expensive United States. Most of my coworkers have families and need the basic health insurance plan UC Davis offers. Others, like the cooks, are either at the beginning of their careers or near the end and want to slow down the pace. There are newly-graduated UC Davis students in managerial positions but also working menial jobs. Surprisingly, Ronny, the dishwasher, is a recent grad.

It really shocks me to learn that a UC Davis alum works as a dishwasher. Hearing about Ronny inspires me to dig more into people's lives. I love hearing my coworkers' stories and this becomes my subject of study. It's a perfect way for me to pass the time while waiting for HR's decision on the managerial position as I watch coffee. My colleagues are super friendly and happy to tell me their stories.

I even get to know why Ronny took the dishwashing gig. He says that sometimes life overwhelms him and he needs to take a break and regroup. I can definitely relate! Ronny took on this dishwasher job just so he could pay his bills—and clear his head. He, a talented writer and a college graduate, washing dishes. Society might consider Ronny a loser. But I don't. He's a man with a plan. I think of Ronny as a person determined to climb the career ladder, no matter what. Even if he has to scrub pots, pans, cups and plates.

Is Ronny going to reach his American Dream? Does he even have one? These questions have bothered me since I met him. But Ronny clarifies his situation for me. "Maggie, I just applied for my PhD in creative writing," he confesses during one of our breaks. I'm thrilled that Ronny is ready to move forward. It truly makes me happy.

In direct opposition to Ronny is Katlyn, a UC Davis graduate who has the front of the house manager position in our dining room. It's encouraging to see a young female get a management job right at the start of her career, and in a highly-regarded educational institution like UC Davis. Spending time with this energetic, young woman, a consummate professional with a bubbly personality, makes my day go faster. Katlyn's liveliness awakens the naughty child in me.

To offset Katlyn's bubbliness is Lora, who oversees the beverage station on the morning shift. (I work the late shift.) Lora always shows up to work dragging her tail and is so miserable she brings everyone else down. Over 40, she's disappointed with her life and depressed. She only recently realized the mistakes she's made. One of them is gambling and another is abusing alcohol. Lora is trying hard to stay away from both addictions. How? By taking on more hours. This makes her not only even more miserable but tired too.

Although Lora works more, she takes home the same money because she has to pay more in taxes. *She works more for less instead of less for more,* is what comes to mind when I think of Lora. One day, I get the nerve to tell her, "You should work less for more money, not the other way around!" But she doesn't get it.

Many of my coworkers love to travel, so much sp that they take any available job to save up for their vacation fantasies. That's another kind of American Dream, I guess. They end up at UC Davis, hired by an independent hospitality company that pays almost double what UC Davis employees make. Then they quit and take a trip.

There's a mix of regular UC Davis workers and those hired from the outside here. The rules to be hired directly by the college are complicated. I discover that seniority comes first and foremost. There's also a union. But as a relatively new UC Davis employee, I'm not sure I'll ever get "membership" to either the seniority or union club. I don't fit into the UC Davis cliques and it doesn't look as though I'll work in their vegan kitchen. They don't have the option of *just* being a vegan cook.

Oh, and I ultimately lose the manager position…to an older, white man. And on top of all this, I discover that something horrific is happening on campus.

•

One beautiful afternoon, right after I start my shift, a colleague stops by my station for a little chat. Bailey mentions a friend who works at UC Davis's primate center. Primate center? I never knew there was such a thing. The primate center is where they keep monkeys to be used for research. "Used" is a nice way to say kill and torture. Bailey's friend ended up quitting his job because he couldn't take the cruelty of raising animals to be sacrificed for medical testing.

At first, I couldn't believe what Bailey tells me but after some research, I see that she's right. Google "California National Primate Research Center" and you'll learn that UC Davis is one of the largest primate centers in California. They house more than 4,700 rhesus, macaque and titi monkeys, from the unborn to the very aged.

Some of the primate center's "research" can truly be called torture. For example, they drill into a monkey's brain to inject chips, which are often infected. A lot of the time, their equipment breaks, which inflicts even more pain on them. UC Davis has been committing these horrendous acts for more than 60 years, since 1962. They manage to keep what they do hidden from the public eye. But since Bailey's friend worked at the lab, he knew the truth—that UC DAVIS, one of the most recognized colleges in the country, conducts cruel experiments on animals.

In fact, UC Davis runs one of the nation's seven National Primate Research Centers, which were established in the 1960s by the National Institute of Health. In 2022, UC Davis reported that they had 8,951 animals in their care, including 5,190 primates. It's one of the biggest animal test centers in the United States. Among the other creatures held captive there are pigs, mice and many others, kept in horrible living conditions. Some have never seen daylight. Many are innoculated with diseases or damaged psychologically; many have lost their lives because of this. Still, UC Davis continues their deadly experiments.

Chapter Thirteen - New Dream, New Destination

What's more, these countless unnecessary tests and experiments inflicted upon helpless are funded by the US government. They invest between five and nine billion dollars in animal research every year. I think UC Davis students and parents should be aware of what goes on in the learning institution where they pay tuition.

After Bailey tells me about the primate center, I stand there with my mouth open, shocked to learn the truth. Now I know the reason I ended up at UC Davis—it's to accomplish something important; to make my mark as an animal activist. Getting a position as a cook, manager or chasing my American Dream doesn't matter anymore. Once again, I'm reminded of my higher purpose. And it is much more than personal success. It's to help these helpless beings.

A few years ago, when I became a certified yoga instructor, I took a pause to reevaluate my life. I see that not much has changed since then, though. I'm in such a panic to make a living, I'm running in circles. I'm chasing the unattainable.

But when I open my eyes this time, I know that my fight against UC Davis's cruelty to animals will become my purpose, my goal, my manifesto. I vow to do as much as I can to save these powerless creatures.

I start by spearheading a protest involving animal rights activists and students. It will happen a few weeks from now. It's us against the UC Davis Primate Center. Will the college fire me? What about my First Amendment Rights? We shall soon see.

I vow to quit my job after the protest but until then, I take advantage of being here to inform people about the tragedy that is happening right under our noses, within UC Davis's walls. Animals are suffering and we are their voice.

Every day, I drive to different campus parking lots, distributing PETA flyers and other animal rights materials. I'm getting ready for the fight. Are you?

I finally figured it out:

My American Dream is for animals in the United States, and beyond, to be free, no matter what the future holds for me.

Epilogue

As time goes on, I become more involved in animal activism, protesting as much as possible. To earn a living, I teach yoga and vegan cooking classes. My dream is to become a vegan consultant. I wish to combine my experience in hospitality, the culinary arts and yoga to teach people how to contribute to the world in a meaningful fashion.

I live by the credo, "Think globally, act locally." It's become my mantra. I firmly believe that as individuals, we can all make change and make a profound connection. As Mahatma Gandhi said, "Be the change you wish to see in the world."

I am.

How about you?

Acknowledgements

Special thanks to my wife, Robin. She introduced me to the vegan/animal activist world and has helped me to grow in vegan society. Robin always stands by my side, in laughter and in tears. She always gently pushes me forward to follow my dreams. She believes that one day, they will come true. I do too …with Robin by my side.

I'd also like to thank my editor Catherine Gigante-Brown for helping me gently wrestle this book into submission and for dotting my I's and crossing my T's.

About the Author

Malgorzata "Maggie" Zurowska was born in Poland. In 2002, she came to the United States in search of adventure. Before her vegan and yogi life, she taught culinary classes as well as courses in tourism and hospitality in New York. During that time, she contributed a chapter on lizard soup to Jonathan Deutsch and Natalya Murakhver's book *They Eat That?: A Cultural Encyclopedia of Weird and Exotic Food from around the World.* In 2016, Maggie self-published her first book, *Sex and Yoga*, a memoir about her New York City life and her travels around the world. She currently lives in Sacramento, California with her wife Robin and many animals. Maggie teaches yoga, vegan cooking classes and how to live a healthy, responsible lifestyle.

Visit Maggie's website:
www.v-karma.com

Milton Keynes UK
Ingram Content Group UK Ltd.
UKHW030347240824
447344UK00001BA/37

9 781963 359152